CONFLICT OF INTEREST: THE ETHICAL DILEMMA IN POLITICS

For Odell and Ken

Conflict of Interest: the Ethical Dilemma in Politics

SANDRA WILLIAMS
Formerly Lecturer in Government,
Bedford College,
University of London

Gower

Published by

Gower Publishing Company Limited,
Gower House, Croft Road,
Aldershot, Hants GU11 3HR, England.

Gower Publishing Company,
Old Post Road,
Brookfield,
Vermont 05036, USA.

British Library Cataloguing in Publication Data

Williams, Sandra
Conflict of interest : the ethical dilemma in politics.
1. Great Britain, *Parliament, House of Commons*
2. Legislators—Great Britain 3. Conflict of interests (Public Office)—Great Britain
I. Title
328.41'073 JN677

ISBN 0-566-00852-1

Printed and bound in Great Britain by
Biddles Ltd, Guildford and King's Lynn

Contents

Tables

Abbreviations

col(s).	column number(s)
Con.	Conservative
CJ	Journal of the House of Commons
Cm(n)d.	Command Paper
EDM	Early Day Motion
HC (followed by a number)	House of Commons Paper
HC Debs (*Parl Debs*)	Parliamentary Debates: House of Commons (*Hansard*)
Hon.	Honourable
Lab.	Labour
Lib.	Liberal
MP	Member of Parliament
PLP	Parliamentary Labour Party
PQ	Parliamentary Question
PR	Public Relations
PRO	Public Record Office
SNP	Scottish National Party
UU	Ulster Unionist
UUUC	United Ulster Unionist Council
Vol.	Volume

Acknowledgements

In the course of writing this study I received help from a very large number of people. Although their assistance was of immeasurable value, it is impossible to acknowledge them all individually. Indeed some, mainly senior civil servants, wish to remain anonymous. However, my special thanks go to Mr. Kenneth Bradshaw, Clerk of the House of Commons (Clerk to the 1969 Select Committee on Members' Interests); Mr. R.S. Lankester, current Registrar of Members' Interests; Mr. D.A.M. Pring, Clerk of the Committees (former Registrar of Members' Interests); and the Rt. Hon. J. Enoch Powell, the first MP to refuse to comply with the registration requirement of the House. They not only gave me the benefit of their time and assistance during the collection of data for the doctoral thesis on which this book is based, but also found the time to read through early draft chapters.

I should also like to express my thanks to Lord Avebury (formerly Eric Lubbock, Liberal member of the 1969 Select Committee on Members' Interests), the Rt. Hon. Michael Foot, Lord Glenamara (formerly the Rt. Hon. E. Short, Chairman of the Labour Party subcommittee on Members' Interests), Lord Houghton of Sowerby (formerly the Rt. Hon. Douglas Houghton, member of the Salmon Commission and a former Chairman of the PLP), Lord Peart, Andrew Roth, Lord Strauss (Chairman of the 1969 Select Committee on Members' Interests), the Rt. Hon. F. Willey (Chairman of the 1974 Select Committee on Members' Interests), Mr. C.B. Winnifrith (Clerk to the 1974 Select Committee on Members' Interests), and to the thirty MPs who kindly took part in my sample survey; all of whom provided me with valuable insights into the experiences of the House of Commons in tackling the problem of conflict of interest. Those acknowledged are, however, disassociated from any interpretations or conclusions drawn in the text. Responsibility for the content of the study is entirely mine. I apologise to the female Members in my sample for using the masculine gender throughout; a stylistic convention but also sadly reflecting the current under-representation of women in the House of Commons.

On editorial issues my appreciation goes to David Hill, my editor, for his early advice and guidance and to Professor Stuart Walkland, University of Sheffield, who was kind enough to read through and comment on a manuscript of this book. Also Andrew Imlach, Editor of Publications, the Commonwealth Parliamentary Association, for his comments, particularly on the American chapter, and for his permission to reprint material from my article in *The Parliamentarian* (Vol. LXIV, July 1983). I am also grateful to the Congressional staff and Congressmen, and staff of the American Embassy Library in London, whose information and advice made the inclusion of an American dimension possible. Finally, for general help and encouragement, my thanks go to Gavin Drewry, Ron Pluck and Margot Jefferys, former tutors and then colleagues at Bedford College, University of London; Bernadette O'Keeffe of King's College London; and to Michael for his patience and support.

Sandra Williams
London
August 1984

1 Introduction: Studying Conflict of Interest

Conflict of interest poses an ethical conundrum for elected and appointed officials. Over the last decade, more than ever before, democratic governments have become anxious about this subject, and have sought a solution to the problem of conflict of interest. Initially concern focused on the executive branch of government, but increasingly, embarrassing revelations have forced legislatures to consider putting their own house in order. The fact that definition and regulation have largely eluded them has major implications for contemporary politics.

Aims and Objectives

The primary aim of this book is to set out and clarify the problem of conflict of interest in representative democracies, and to examine different ways of tackling the problem. The focus is on the legislative arm in politics and, in particular, the British House of Commons.

Actual or apparent conflict, or convergence, of public duty with private interest has been the cause of many scandals for those in the public eye, occasionally with serious repercussions. Chapter 2 of this study confronts the conundrum head on and asks, what is the problem of conflict of interest in public life? It examines the aims and objectives of conflict of interest regulations and draws out the special features which differentiate the problem of conflict of interest in the legislative from that in the executive branch of government.

The main empirical case study which follows examines the hitherto undocumented experience of the British House of Commons in dealing with the problem of conflict of interest on the part of Members. It is based on research undertaken for my Ph.D. thesis on the same subject[1], and draws heavily on both documentary sources (House of Commons Debates, Parliamentary Questions, Early Day Motions and Select Committee Reports), and on conversations I had with MPs and House of Commons staff from 1978 to 1980; either as part of a random sample survey of Members, or because they were individuals with specific knowledge on the Members' interest debate.[2] Although the practice of the House of Commons, with its reliance on parliamentary tradition and a minimum of written rules, does not necessarily provide the blueprint for others to follow, it gives insight into what is possible and what difficulties are likely to be encountered in tackling the problem of conflict of interest. The case study does not extend to the House of Lords where there are no strict rules covering the pecuniary interests of peers when they are acting in their parliamentary capacity, simply personal honour and convention referred to in standing orders. Throughout my use of the term Parliament is therefore restricted to the House of Commons.

Chapter 7 compares Parliament's approach to that imposed on local government and the home civil service, and examines the charge of differing standards. Has Parliament been less thorough and effective in putting its own House in order than it has been in making or recommending standards for others to keep?

In Chapter 8 the comparison moves to international ground and the traditional approach of the House is contrasted with the more codified rules of the American Congress, which incorporate conflict of interest statutes. It draws both on the Official Record, and on information and perceptions provided by Congressmen and congressional staff. A general criticism has been raised that the question of international comparison is distorted by such contrasts with the United States, as the constitutional arrangements of the United States make Congress a special case. Instead comparison is made with other parliamentary systems where the constitutional relationship between the legislature and executive is comparable with Britain's.[3] However, it is precisely because the various constitutional arrangements of diverse political systems create different opportunities for conflict of interest, and therefore might require different approaches to the question of restraints, that the US Congress has been included in this study. The aim is both to highlight the uniquely British experience of the House of Commons, and to illustrate alternative methods of curbing conflict of interest.

Finally, the problem of conflict of interest in representative democracies is reappraised, and a synopsis provided of the factors to be taken into account in formulating conflict of interest provisions for legislatures. Conflict of interest is not an occasional aberration in the democratic system, but an inherent flaw. Some conflicts, or convergences, of interests are inevitable in a representative democracy.

Studying Conflict of Interest

A major criticism of much parliamentary literature is that it emphasises description of observable events as the ultimate goal, and lacks conceptual analysis or theoretical content; a fault which is symptomatic of the empirical–normative distinction in political science.[4] The fundamental methodological premise of this study is that such a distinction is invalid, and that a more rewarding approach would be to bridge this empirical–normative divide by emphasising the *relationship* between values, institutions and behaviour in society. Hence, in addition to observable events, the facts to be explored and interpreted include cultural values and ideals which shape both the aims and objectives of those involved in regulating conflict of interest, and the means by which this goal is pursued. In this respect the inquiry has a conscious affinity with Max Weber's prescription for the tasks of an empirical science.[5]

The inclusion of beliefs and values in the equation should not, however, be interpreted as affording culture, or the narrower dimension of ideology, an unqualified role as an independent variable in influencing social development. Although there is an intervening variable between people and objective situations – that is, culture – any attempt to explain behaviour solely in terms of cultural values comes up against the problem of 'social inertia'.[6] Culture is not a static concept and has to be created anew in each generation. To take values or norms as a starting point in analysis, without considering the aspect of transmission and maintenance, overlooks the possibility that values do in fact alter in response to circumstance.

Correspondingly, behaviour is viewed here as 'a function of both *environmental situations* in which actors find themselves and the *psychological predispositions* they bring to these situations'.[7] Attitudes and situations can be seen as operating in a kind of push–pull relationship, 'the stronger the attitudinal press for a course of action, the less need for situational stimuli and vice versa'.[8] This view of behaviour need not, however, involve a psychological explanation because both sets of conditions governing behaviour can be seen as given to the individual by society.

The implication of this approach for the case study of the House of Commons is that in addition to exploring 'environmental factors', on the assumption that Parliament does not operate in a vacuum, this inquiry examines the beliefs, values and habits of thought which have built up over time and which guide and inform Members' action and behaviour towards outside financial interests and the associated problem of conflict of interest. These politically relevant beliefs, values and habits of thought can be grouped together under the rubric of 'élite political culture'. Bearing in mind the historical and cumulative basis of culture, I argue that the approach of Members towards the problem of conflict of interest derives as much from historical residues of élite political culture as from functional considerations and contemporary pressures.[9]

My approach challenges the view of some writers, including Harold Laski, that the ideal of the 'gentleman'[10] has become redundant as a working hypothesis in political research. The experience of the House of Commons in dealing with conflict of interest suggests that various facets of this composite ideal, such as honour, self-restraint, loyalty, mutual trust, the belief in politics as an amateur pursuit and the associated tradition of part-time membership of the House, do still provide a pattern and example for many MPs, although they themselves are unlikely to identify or describe their behaviour in these terms. However, conflict of interest is regarded by Parliaments and governments as a 'House' issue rather than a 'party' issue, and one which concerns internal discipline of Members rather than the formulation of public policy. On such matters Parliaments and governments tend to be peculiarly introverted, with debate becoming submerged in issues of political ethics and parliamentary manners. It is likely therefore that while the idea of the 'gentleman' is a useful heuristic device in this and other domestic contexts, it is less illuminative of the House's performance in the wider arena of public policy-making. Indeed, an introverted preoccupation with 'House' matters may be regarded as an anodyne to sooth painful awareness of lack of influence in matters of public policy.

In as much as action and behaviour are shaped by functional considerations and contemporary pressures of the environmental situation in which actors find themselves, the 'issue-attention cycle' model also proved a useful device for initiating and structuring an analysis of conflict of interest regulation. Variants of this model have in the main been developed in a number of American studies concerned with environmental problems.[11] The potential usefulness of the model is also gradually being recognised in the more general field of social policy research, where it has been used to explore the 'emergence' or 'non-emergence' of issues on the political agenda, as opposed to the processing of issues that have already emerged.[12] In this context it has been linked with the concept of 'nondecision-making', which is integral to a school of thought subscribed to by this study, which holds that the failure of an élite to act or make decisions is often of greater importance than the decisions they make. This belief involves what Steven Lukes calls a 'two-dimensional' view of power,[13] with both decision-making and nondecision-making viewed as proper objects of investigation. Nondecision-making can in itself be a manifestation of bias in a political system.

The dynamics of the 'issue-attention cycle' model reflect 'a systematic cycle of heightening public interest and then increasing boredom with major issues'.[14] Applying this model more specifically to issues involving the reform of the governmental operation or procedure, and implying that reform is usually a transient phenomenon in a political system ordinarily resistant to change, Francis Rourke has given the following description of the cycle:

> As a general rule the public is not greatly interested in such questions and is aroused from its indifference only when scandalous misconduct by an officeholder is suddenly revealed. Dramatic exposure of wrongdoing usually does excite widespread public interest and, while it persists, the prospect for reform of the political process brightens if the wrongdoing can be linked to some basic defect in the system. But this support for change commonly recedes as the impact of the scandal wears off, and members of the public return to their customary private concerns.[15]

Rourke's formulation of the cycle is at the core of the 'issue-attention cycle' model used in this study as a base on which to structure and initiate an analysis of the House of Common's approach to conflict of interest regulation. In practice, given the dual components of behaviour, no stage of the cycle, with its emphasis on contemporary events, can be understood in isolation from the beliefs, values and habits of the actors involved.

2 The Problem of Conflict of Interest in Representative Democracies

Towards a Definition

A book about conflict of interest presupposes at least a rudimentary idea of what constitutes conflict of interest and where it ends and some other phenomenon begins. Definitions of conflict of interest used by political commentators vary in format, but at the heart of most is the notion that conflict of interest denotes 'a situation in which an official has a private financial interest sufficient to influence, or appear to influence, the exercise of his public duties and responsibilities'. The concept is applicable not only to situations where a conflict *actually* exists, but also where it *appears* to exist. A charge of conflict of interest may arise not only when public duty clashes with private interest, but also when they appear to converge.

This conflict or convergence is invariably reduced to two specific interests: the interest of the elected or appointed public official in the proper administration of his office; and his interest in his own private financial affairs. The official's personal interest is usually defined in narrow pecuniary terms because it would be difficult to identify and regulate other rewards, psychological or emotional ones for example, which might influence an individual's action. This view is illustrated by James Kirby who, in explaining why the Association of the Bar of the City of New York singled out economic ties in its study of congressional ethics, endorsed the argument of a predecessor committee that:

> The simplest reason is that it is better to control whatever fraction of improper behaviour is attributable to economic motives than to control none. The second reason is that regulatory schemes can be written with reasonable particularity and enforced with moderate predictability; no one has yet devised a method for sorting out acquaintances, friends, relations, and lovers for the purposes of a rule permitting official dealings with some and not with others.[1]

Emotional sentiments and environmental conditioning are bound to influence the decision-making of those in public life, but only a fraction of the total possible pressures and relationships which shape their decisions are amenable to conflict of interest regulations. While this concentration on pecuniary benefits can therefore be defended on practical grounds, it cannot avoid the fact that even if no financial gain accrues to the official involved, other aspects of the conflict of interest dilemma do create problems and attract criticism. For example, as we will see when looking at the British Parliament and the American Congress, the problem of competition for the Member's time has been recognised. While the customary argument against Members pursuing business interests focuses on the potential business bias in the House, there is also the criticism that a multiplicity of outside interests may pre-empt an unduly large amount of the time and energy MPs have available to think about and perform their public duties.

Public duty vs. private interests: a false dichotomy?

The deceptive simplicity of a definition based on conflict between public duty and private interests should not obscure the fact that conflict of interest is an ethical conundrum both for the elected and appointed officials concerned, and for those involved in devising safeguards against such conflict; in the case of Parliament and Congress these being largely one and the same body. The ambiguities which attach to the concept increase when the focus moves from abstract definition to real events in public life.

Drawing a clear distinction between an official's private interests and his public duty involves a universal assumption of 'depersonalisation' of public office which is popular in organisational theory, but often a chimera in the everyday workings of public life. It also implies a neat separation between the proper administration of the official's office and his interest in his private economic affairs which is not easy to achieve in practice. The increasingly complex nature of government and society, along with the growth of the public sector, enables the government–non-government dichotomy to be maintained in very few sectors of activity, and as Robert Getz has observed, 'by far the greatest area is one with shades of grey between what is purely governmental and what is purely private'.[2]

Ultimately the feasibility of conflict of interest restraints fashioned on the dichotomy between public interest and private duty hinge on a philosophical imponderable: that is whether man is basically altruistic and willing to sacrifice his own ends for the public interest or some other larger good, or whether the tendency of man is to take advantage of all available means to further his own privileges. Do we expect public officials to make an objective distinction and absolute segregation between private interests and public duty, or do we accept Cornelius O'Leary's conclusion, reached in the light of his study of electoral corruption, that 'to attempt to divorce personal interests completely from political activity would be to strive after the unattainable'?[3] Perhaps some insight into this dilemma is contained in the following comment by a former civil servant at the Property Services Agency, found guilty of accepting bribes (a vacuum cleaner, a car jack and a lady of ill-repute). Asked by a *TV Eye* reporter, 'why did you do it?' he replied, 'I'm a man like you, I'm a human being' (*TV Eye*, ITV, January 1984).

'Interests' in politics

The conflict of interest dilemma is aggravated by the ambiguous use of the term 'interest' in politics and here we would be well advised to bear in mind E.E. Schattschneider's observation that in politics the whole discussion of interests is subjective:

> All discussions of interests, special as well as general, refer to motives, desires and intentions of people. In this sense the whole discussion of interests is subjective. We have made progress in the study of politics because people have observed some kind of relation between the political behaviour of people and certain wholly impersonal data concerning their ownership of property, income, economic status, professions and the like. All that we know about interests, private as well as public, is based on inferences of this sort. Whether the distinction in any given case is valid depends on the evidence and on kinds of inferences drawn from the evidence.[4]

Discussion about interests in politics involves normative judgments of a moral and political character, so as Steven Lukes explains, it should be no surprise that different opinions of what interests *are* are associated with different moral and political opinions.[5]

The scope of private interests considered relevant to the conflict of interest debate also varies, extending from the fundamental level of interests the official possesses while holding office to encompass interests discarded when taking office, interests their families have and interests acquired on leaving office. Concern about British MPs and conflict of interest has tended to focus on interests possessed by themselves and their families while holding office, but when we look at Ministers and at other sectors of the public service it becomes increasingly necessary to take into account the controversy surrounding the acquisition of economic interests on leaving office. This is most likely to arise with Ministers and senior civil servants on retirement or resignation, where there are potential opportunities for using confidential information or expertise obtained in Whitehall, or influencing policy either for their own benefit or for that of their prospective employers.

Problems surrounding the identification and regulation of private interests will become obvious in later chapters. However, definitions of conflict of interest also tend to incorporate some notion of the 'public interest' and the reader should be alert to the chameleon-like qualities of this concept, called a 'social fiction' by Samuel Finer because 'everybody agrees that it exists but nobody knows wherein it consists'.[6] In exploring the conundrum of conflict of interest we must ask ourselves whether we are dealing with an objective 'public interest' as something of substance apart from the clash of personal and group interests or whether, as Professor George Jones argues, such a conception of public interest is 'inappropriate in a political system which emphasises pluralistic bargaining between groups as the way to uncover the public interest'.[7]

The additional problem of a self-interested interpretation of 'public interest' in politics also has to be reckoned with. Consciously or not, politicians frequently equate the public with what suits them and their associates, a fact Disraeli recognised when he remarked,

> . . . as in private life we are accustomed to associate the circle of our acquaintance with the phrase 'the world', so in public I have invariably observed that 'the people' of the politician is the circle of his interests.[8]

The representative dimension

In this study we are primarily concerned with conflict of interest and *elected* as opposed to appointed officials. In this context, the concept of 'interest(s)' takes on extra dimensions. Here we have to take into account the nature of the representative function of the Member and the unique qualities of legislative employment. A Member of Parliament, for example, is properly subject to a number of outside interests and influences which may induce him to ask parliamentary questions, speak or vote a certain way in the House, table amendments to legislation, contact Ministers and so on. A major problem, therefore, with identifying and regulating conflict of interest in legislatures is deciding just where representation of interests threatens to cross the fine, some may say invisible, line into a conflict of interest situation. This is all the more complicated by the fact that activities which in one country are considered as a normal part of representation (for example, the practice of individual MPs being supported by trade unions or businesses) may be viewed as an unacceptable conflict of interest in another. The question is whether there is any evidence that private interests have improperly influenced political activity or that political positions have been used for private gain.

What constitutes an unacceptable conflict of interest as distinct from an acceptable representation of interests hinges largely on a prior conception of the proper representative function of the legislator, but this has changed over time and the literature on representation is full of obvious disagreements over its meaning. Frustration with the lack of clarity in representation theory has led some commentators to put 'normative speculation' on one side and to undertake empirical investigation of what representatives actually do.[9] Regrettably, the ambivalent and varied interpretations of the representative role of the British MP provided by the MPs in my sample survey bear out the view that, 'empirical investigation is no less ambiguous in its results than the traditional "normative" controversy'.[10] MPs frequently and indiscriminantly mix up the stylistic and focal dimensions of representation between which they should in fact distinguish. Analytically, although not necessarily in practice, the style of representation is neutral as regards the focus of representation.[11] The latter, regardless of whether it is a geographical unit, a pressure group, a party or a personal interest, does not commit the representative to adopting either the style of an independent trustee or the style of a mandated delegate.

Conflicts inherent in representative government

Furthermore, it has to be recognised that some conflicts of interests are inherent in a representative system of government and are not necessarily wrong or unethical. For example, although more common in America than in Britain where the majority of MPs do not represent perfectly homogenous constituencies, an unavoidable conflict can arise between an MP's fiduciary obligations, which require the separation of private interests from public duties, and his representative duties. Constituents, or more accurately local party officials, may choose a prospective candidate largely because he has a personal interest which coincides with theirs, as in the case of a farmer chosen to represent an agricultural community or a business man adopted to represent a commercial area. Unavoidably, in representing his constituents, a

Member may here be seen as working on his own behalf, or promoting his private interests and of violating his fiduciary duty.

A more general confirmation of the conflicts inherent in the legislator's role is evident when we remember that an MP does not work in isolation, but operates with other representatives in an institutionalised context with the principal goal of governing the nation. Hanna Pitkin has described how local or partial interests constantly vie with the 'national interest' because 'politics entails the reconciliation of conflicting claims, each usually with some justice on its side; the harmony of final-objective-interests must be created'.[12] This view was illustrated for me by a Conservative Member of the British House of Commons included in my sample survey, who saw the major function of an MP to be precisely that of reconciling conflicts of interest. He argued that 'as an elected representative an MP is constantly having to weigh up the interests of his country, his constituency, his party outside the House nationally and locally, his party inside the House and sectional interests'. These foci of representation are never all in harmony and there are endless permutations.

Moreover, as the case study of the House of Commons illustrates, the controversial activity of legislators representing personal or sectional interests need not be against the spirit of the House. Representatives who possess outside personal or sectional interests – for example pressure group connections, business affiliations, trade union sponsorship – often justify this activity in terms of the advantage to be gained by the House in terms of the quality of debate. One enthusiastic supporter of outside interests included in my sample survey went so far as to claim that 'the British House of Commons derives strength from the outside interests of Members and until the whole structure is reformed, good government rests on the practical experience of MPs'.

Such practical experience and information is frequently acquired through consultation with a myriad of interest groups which seek to influence the process of government and this has now become an integral and accepted part of both the British and the American political systems. As J.D. Stewart reasons, this relationship between MPs and groups is acceptable and indeed valuable if an MP is to play a useful part in the affairs of his country, even if financial considerations are involved, so long as the connection is known and *both* the MP and the group have the freedom to enter and terminate the relationship.[13] What is not acceptable is for such a relationship to be deliberately concealed, or for the MP either to compromise his independence by his association with an outside interest, or to turn his advisory role into one of *advocating* in the House interests with which he may have a financial connection. If we accept the premise that MPs' representing personal and sectional interests is part of the unavoidable reality of our political system as currently constituted, then conflict of interest hinges primarily on the stylistic dimension of representation.

Conflict of interest overlaps with corruption

Confusion and ambiguity over what constitutes conflict of interest in public life is heightened by the erroneous belief that conflict of interest can be treated as a weak form of the more emotionally charged phenomenon of corruption. This error is unfortunately perpetuated by those whose intention, paradoxically, is to clarify the concept. Clement Vose, for example, in describing the etymology of conflict of interest in the *International Encyclopaedia of the Social Sciences* states:

> In the nineteenth century, if an official resolved a clash between his personal advantage and public duty in favour of personal advantage it was called corruption, . . . since then 'corruption' has come to be associated with only the most odious and obvious forms of venality and self-service and the term 'conflict of interest' was coined to cover less blatant cases.

Corruption is referred to in a variety of contexts but here we are primarily concerned with the overlap between conflict of interest and corruption within the state, namely political corruption. Like conflict of interest, corruption has proved difficult to define. In Britain legal definitions are embodied in the three Acts collectively known as the Prevention of Corruption Acts, which have in turn been reinterpreted by the courts. Their effect on the public sector is not consistent. The Public Bodies Corrupt Practices Act, 1889 applies to local government and other local public bodies. It is not applicable to Crown servants or the private sector. The Prevention of Corruption Act, 1906 applies to any person employed by or acting for another in the public and private sectors and specifically includes Crown Servants. The 1889 Act makes it an offence for anyone 'corruptly to give or receive any gift or other advantage as an inducement to influence the conduct of any member, officer or servant of any public body as defined in the Act' (Salmon Commission Cmnd 6524, para 44). The 1906 Act makes it an offence for any gift or consideration to be corruptly offered or received as an inducement to influence an 'agent's' conduct in relation to his principal's affairs or business. The Prevention of Corruption Act, 1916 extended the definition of 'public body' in the 1889 Act to include 'local and Public authorities of all descriptions' and increased the penalties under the two previous Acts for offences involving contracts with public bodies or Government departments. It also introduced the new aspect of 'presumption of corruption' where anyone seeking a contract from a Government department or public body gave any 'money, gift or other consideration' to any government employee.

Thus the onus changed, and it became up to the *defence* to prove that the gift or consideration was not given or received corruptly.

The offence of corruption as defined by these Acts consists of three main ingredients. It has to be shown:

(1) that a gift or consideration was given or offered by one party to another;
(2) that the gift or consideration was given, or received, as an *inducement* or *reward* for services to be rendered or already rendered in relation to official duties; and
(3) that the transaction took place corruptly.
(Salmon Commission Cmnd 6524: 1976, para 51)

The statutory definition of corruption does not attempt to be exhaustive and rests on the implicit premise that it is preferable for judges to construct definitions incrementally by way of litigation; a process which is to some extent responsive to the nuances of changing mores.

The legal concept of corruption applies only to the most flagrant practices which have been the subject of adverse judicial decisions and is not broad enough to cover the concept as seen from the viewpoints of political science and ethics. Consequently, within the social sciences several broader definitions of political corruption have developed, each utilising different criteria:

(1) public office centred definition – establishing a concept of public office and labelling as corruption deviations from standards of conduct binding upon incumbents.[14]
(2) market centred definitions – in terms of theory of the market whereby the public servant regards his public office as a business and seeks to maximise his income, the size of which depends 'upon the market situation and his talent for finding the point of maximal gain on the public's demand curve'.[15]
(3) public interest definition – corruption is seen as a subversion of 'public interest'.[16]

All of these definitions involve ambiguities. Definitions (1) and (2) involve asking which norms are to be used to distinguish corrupt from non-corrupt acts, whilst definition (3) utilises the indeterminant concept of 'public interest'. Thus, while precision and clarity regarding corruption are difficult to obtain even within the relatively limited boundaries of law, once outside these boundaries we are once again caught up in a maze of conflicting moral opinion.

The vagueness of the concept of corruption in part accounts for the ease with which allegations of conflict of interest can escalate into accusations of corruption in the excitement of a political scandal. Talking with Members of the British Parliament illustrated just how

Table 1

MPs' views on what constitutes corruption

What does respondent understand by the term corruption?	Total Sample %
Respondent emphasised:	
Legal aspect; i.e. dishonest practice for money	40.00
Conflict of interest; i.e. where personal financial interest overcomes or distorts Member's public duty as MP.	36.67
Benefit to Member or other; i.e. doing something for one's own advantage or to the advantage of someone else for money, position or benefit in kind.	13.33
Moral as well as pecuniary aspect of corruption	10.00

Table 2

MPs' views on how far conflict of interest overlaps with corruption

Views on how far conflict of interest overlaps with corruption	Total Sample %
Totally different terms; corruption associated with behaviour for personal financial gain, whereas conflict of interest need have no connotation of personal gain and in a non-pecuniary sense is endemic to politics.	26.67
Potentially overlapping terms; conflict of interest may arise innocently but could be resolved in a corrupt way.	36.67
Overlapping terms; no strict demarcation between the two terms. Both conflict of interest and corruption loosely defined as conflict between private interest and public duty with conflict of interest shading off into corruption.	26.67
Other	6.67
Do not know	3.33

often in political life the term is indiscriminately interchanged with corruption. I asked the 30 MPs included in my sample survey what they understood by the term 'corruption', and followed this up by asking them how far it overlapped, if at all, with 'conflict of interest'. Their responses varied greatly, but it was possible to reduce them to the very general categories summarised in Tables 1 and 2.

As can be seen from Table 1, 40 per cent of Members interviewed referred to the legal definition of corruption embodied in criminal law. They rarely mentioned the Prevention of Corruption Acts directly but used such phrases as 'doing something dishonest for money' or 'the taking of payment in the furtherance of a cause which might be judged illegal'. Among these responses corruption was frequently associated with bribery, the one specific financial connection not tolerated by the House and which has been proscribed by a resolution of the House since 1695.

The ingredient of conflict of interest in the definition of corruption was emphasised by approximately 37 per cent of Members. However, for them it was not sufficient for conflict of interest simply to exist. Corruption arises only where personal financial interest overcomes or distorts a Member's duty as an MP. Closely associated with this category of response, although not directly picking out the actual conflict of interest element, were those attempts at definition which stressed the act of doing something for one's own advantage or to the advantage of someone else, not just for money, but for position or benefit in kind. Lastly, 10 per cent of Members stressed that people, and in this specific instance MPs, can be morally corrupted as well as financially corrupted. Arguing that 'money is the narrow view' they referred to corruption by drink, immorality and bigotry. Few of the MPs drew a strict demarcation between the two phenomena. Those who did argued that corruption was associated with behaviour for personal gain, whereas conflict of interest need have no connection of personal gain and, as we have seen above, in a non-pecuniary sense is endemic to the representative's role in politics. The majority of MPs either viewed conflict of interest and corruption as potentially overlapping terms, on the grounds that conflict of interest may arise innocently but could be resolved in a corrupt way, or posited a closer relationship between the two, judging that no clear distinction could be made between them. This latter view was summed up by a Conservative MP who commented, 'a conflict of interest is where your judgment as a politician, as an MP, conflicts with your best interests in the financial and business sense. Corruption follows on from this definition of conflict of interest and is where you allow one to overcome the other'. It also underlay the view of the Labour Member who ventured, 'we know the legal definition of corruption, i.e. the buying of a vote or voice on an issue etc.; beyond that it shades off into conflict of interest where it is a matter for the conscience of the individual MP'.

While politicians and commentators alike tend to conflate conflict of interest and corruption in public life, and there is inevitably an intermediary grey area partaking of the quality of both, analytically a distinction should be drawn between the two. Conflict of interest in itself does not imply resolution in favour of personal advantage, merely that a conflict exists which could be resolved in one of several ways. Corruption, on the other hand, can be viewed as a particular method of resolving this conflict, whereby personal financial interest overcomes or distorts the exercise of an official's public duties and responsibilities; distortion may of course be incidentally beneficial to the 'public interest'. Corruption is not an end in itself, simply an illegal means to achieve a particular outcome or effect.

Conflict of interest as a 'negotiated classification of behaviour'

While we can strive for conceptual clarity with terms such as conflict of interest, corruption and representation, and attempt to distinguish between them analytically, the position a writer, or a member, officer or servant of a public body adopts within the limits set by each concept will depend on what Pitkin calls 'his metapolitics – his broad conception of human nature, human society, and political life'.[17] Indeed, it will be shaped and determined by the myriad of life experiences which are embedded in the pattern of his political thought. Thus, conflict of interest can be best thought of not as an 'inherent quality' of behaviour but as a 'negotiated classification' of behaviour, whereby classification of the behaviour is accomplished by the application of certain tacit, common sense interpretive criteria dependent on the particular social context and past experiences of the observer.

This distinction has already been explored by S. Chibnall and P. Saunders with specific reference to the character of corruption.[18] The basis of the argument is that, as with the variety of interpretations of 'interests' in politics, the same act may be amenable to a variety of interpretations because people have different views on a situation or act according to their social context, experiences etc. For example, what is acceptable to one individual may be totally unacceptable to another; and this relates both to the propriety of holding an outside financial interest and to the behaviour of the public official holding such an interest. Further, for those who are implicated in cases of alleged misconduct this often means that at some point they are faced with an unfavourable reclassification by another body, perhaps a select committee, a tribunal of inquiry or even a court, of actions they themselves had perceived as acceptable at the time.

The problem of identifying conflict of interest is not just a matter of fact but also a matter of socially structured perception. In cases of alleged conflict of interest the circumstances of the time, the form and place of the official's action, and the interpretation to be put on the action, as well as the intention of the official are all relative factors and opinion may reasonably differ as to the importance to be attached to each of them. However, recognition of such relativity does not mean that we should abandon altogether attempts at curbing the problem of conflict of interest in public life. While rules and conventions cannot guarantee ethical behaviour, they may at least sharpen the moral decisions of members, officers and servants in the public sector who know that their actions can be judged against the background of such controls.

Conflict of Interest Regulations: Aims and Objectives

Allegations of conflict of interest can have damaging repercussions not just for the personal, professional or political future of the individual involved, but also for the image and effectiveness of the public body to which he belongs. Thus a fundamental long-term goal of conflict of interest regulations is to maintain the actuality and appearance of a high standard of ethical conduct in the public service.

This general aim is pursued by two more immediate objectives. First, conflict of interest rules – corruption legislation aside – are primarily designed to enable the individual to separate his legitimate interests from his public duty. The aim here is to ensure, as far as possible, the independence of public office. Although, as we have argued, conflict of interest provisions cannot guarantee ethical behaviour, a firm and relatively unambiguous set of guidelines, evolved to suit the changing needs of the time, sharpens the moral judgments of those who must exercise their discretion in separating private interests from public duty. Second, the rules are designed not just to avoid the risk of actual conflict of interest with the associated temptation of corruption, but also, where possible, to eliminate even the suspicion or appearance of conflict of interest.

In practice, the achievement of these objectives will be hindered by the several flaws in a definition of conflict of interest fashioned on the dichotomy between private interest and public duty discussed above. It must also be remembered that the majority of conflict of interest restraints are designed to regulate economic ties only, and thus control no more than a small part of the total pressures and relationships which bear on the activities of those engaged in public service.

The majority of conflict of interest provisions can be classified as preventative regulations in that they are intended to regulate potential harm before the conflict occurs, by marking out what situations to avoid. Although they are increasingly being written into formal codes of conduct, they are usually based on a taken-for-granted, informal, unwritten code of ethics, born of the philosophy that public office is a 'public trust'.

Complacency over conflict of interest provisions has, however, been shaken by evidence of wilful violations of expected ethical standards and the result has been a move towards conflict of interest legislation. In America, for example, a legacy of the Watergate affair was the Ethics in Government Act, 1978 (S555–PL 95–521) which codified the disclosure requirements for Congress and top Executive and Judicial branch employees, and enabled civil penalties, particularly fines, to be imposed for wilful violations.

Once formal rules are introduced, however, the problems of enforcement and policing arise, and as we shall see in following chapters, even the most stringent of financial codes of ethics is difficult to enforce in order to achieve the objectives outlined above.

A further consideration is that in the pursuit of ethical conduct the target of avoiding conflict of interest has to be weighed against competing goals, such as the recruitment and morale of those in the public service. As one observer of ethics in American government has remarked,

> ethics in any group arises out of a sense of tradition and pride in his particular calling. Humiliate that group. Subject them to constant restriction and supervision. Refuse to trust them in any of their activities in or out of government and you destroy any possibility of an effective ethical code.[19]

Drafters of conflict of interest provisions have the delicate task of balancing these competing goals.

3 The Tradition of the Financially Independent Member

Rules and conventions are not created in a vacuum, but emerge in response to particular social, economic and political circumstances. Thus in order to explain the peculiarly British response to the problem of conflict of interest, and not simply to catalogue the rules and conventions of the House, we should first consider the changing social, economic and political context from which Members have been recruited and in which they operate.

The range of background information which could be included in this chapter is vast, comprising not only contemporary facts but also, and perhaps more importantly for our purpose of tracing the evolution of rules and conventions, a historical perspective on the culture and composition of the British House of Commons. Detailed studies of political recruitment and socio-economic profiles of MPs over time are already available for the reader to consult.[1] Therefore, we shall focus here on the tradition of the financially independent Member, which is central both to the membership and functioning of Parliament, and to the treatment there of conflict of interest.

This tradition encompasses issues such as the payment of Members, Members' outside interests and the status MPs ascribe to themselves in the parliamentary system (that is, whether membership is seen as part-time or full-time), all of which are essential to understanding the experience of the House of Commons in dealing with conflict of interest. Parliament has traditionally supported and promoted the role of the financially independent Member and consequently in dealing with conflict of interest the House has never questioned the propriety of Members' possessing outside interests, simply the means by which some of these should be disclosed.

Outside Financial Interests vs. Payment of Members

The tradition of Members possessing outside pecuniary interests has always been closely bound up with the controversial question of the payment of Members. The ancient custom of payment of Members by their own electors existed as early as the thirteenth century, when the representatives of the shires, cities and boroughs were remunerated by their constituents for their attendance at Parliament, knights receiving four shillings a day and citizens and burgesses two shillings a day for the term of Parliament. However, during the Tudor period this practice was gradually undermined by the growing number of people who were attracted by the high prestige of a seat in Parliament and were prepared to disclaim their parliamentary wages. Such agreements became increasingly common in the seventeenth century, and by a resolution of the House of Commons, the payment of Members ceased in 1677. The last MP to have received this parliamentary salary is commonly said to have been Andrew Marvell, who was paid by the Borough of Kingston upon Hull until his death in 1678. Membership of Parliament remained an unpaid occupation until 1912, when a payment of £400 was authorised for all Members not receiving salaries as Ministers or Officers of the House.

In the intervening period the tradition of the House of Commons as a meeting place of gentlemen, who saw membership of Parliament as a public service and not a job, became well entrenched, supported by the popular belief that Britain could be governed by gifted amateurs:

> . . . politics was regarded as an amateur pursuit, one which neither demanded a man's entire energies nor aroused so much partisanship as to interfere with the easy social relationship with men of the same class regardless of their politics.[2]

The enthronement of the amateur in government and administration was consolidated by what V. Subramaniam calls the 'two-step democratic evolution in Britain'.[3] The essence of this form of political and historical evolution was the seizure of power from the monarch by an enlightened aristocracy and landed gentry, who established a lay common-sense approach to matters of government and administration *before* the second stage of development – the enlargement and reform of the administrative structure – began in the mid-nineteenth century. The administrative machine was subsequently fashioned in accordance with the assumptions of this tradition.

Belief in politics as an amateur pursuit went hand in hand with the view that service in Parliament ought to be honorary and that Members of Parliament ought to be persons who could pay for the privilege. Members were presumed to live on their own resources and barriers existed to exclude from Parliament those without independent means. For example, by the middle of the eighteenth century enactments had been passed which established the principle that expenses at elections were chargeable to candidates, and in 1710 a property qualification was imposed for membership of the House; a knight of the shire had to possess an income of £600 a year and a borough representative £300, both derived from land. The satirist Swift summed up the Tory enthusiasm for pushing the property qualification through Parliament:

> . . . they have taken care in their first session, by that noble bill of qualification, that future Parliaments should be composed of landed men, and our properties be no more at the mercy of those who have none themselves, or at least what is only transient or imaginary.[4]

Swift's observation on the preservation of landed interests was largely borne out in the social composition of Parliament prior to franchise reform in 1832. Of the 5,034 Members who sat in the House of Commons from 1734 to 1832, at least three-quarters had their chief economic interest in land.[5]

Another factor favouring the entrenchment of the financially independent Member was the far from gentlemanly practice of treating and bribing individual electors in the boroughs, which flourished in the seventeenth century and persisted well into the eighteenth century. This made it virtually impossible for a candidate to enter an election unless he had the wherewithal to secure a seat. Once secured, a seat could itself prove profitable in terms of sinecure offices and pensions. Thus, in the eighteenth century and for much of the nineteenth century, many prospective Members were prepared to pay considerable sums for a seat or courted the patronage of notables who could furnish them with one. The corrupt and surreptitious activity during this period of parliamentary history was colourfully evoked by Peter Alfred Taylor MP in 1870 as grounds for restoring the ancient constitutional custom of payment of Members:

> Payment of Members is the symbol of a system of honest work fairly remunerated, while non-payment symbolises a system which can hardly be more laconically illustrated than by a well-known politician of two generations back, who, in a moment, as I presume, of postprandial candour, thus apostrophised his constituents: 'I bought you, and, by G–, I'll sell you!'[6]

The tradition of the independent Member was not necessarily reflected in eighteenth-century practice in terms of independent action in Parliament. Samuel Beer has described both the representatives of financial interests in Parliament who were anxious to secure contracts for loans, remittances, or perhaps the supply of goods, and the frequency of the patron–nominee relationship which highlighted the economic interests of the patron and conferred a considerable burden of dependence on the MP.[7] However, in the eighteenth century the concept of independence was narrowly interpreted, meaning only independence from the Crown. The form of conflict of interest which the Rockingham Whigs were concerned with was that between the public interest and the interest of royal placemen and pensioners, and it was generally accepted that MPs should be independent from royal influence.

In the eighteenth century the procedure for private bills did not possess the semi-judicial character which it acquired during the nineteenth century and there was much opportunity for the intervention of the interested MP. As Pares has observed, during this century,

> Most . . . legislation was private, local and facultative, setting up local agencies, such as turnpike, paving, enclosure or improvement commissioners where such things appeared to be desired by the preponderant local interests . . . Even legislation which was ostensibly national, imposing customs duties or regulating overseas trade, often had local implications and Members of Parliament handled it as agents of local interests.[8]

Eighteenth-century politics saw nothing wrong in the close connection of an MP with interests being favoured by a Bill in which he was concerned. Indeed, there is much to support Beer's conclusion that the Old Whig theory of representation in the eighteenth century actually condoned the pursuit of personal interests and may have effectively cancelled out what would now be perceived as a conflict of interest. Then MPs were regarded as elected representatives whose primary obligation was not to promote the interests of their electors but to promote the interests of the nation as a whole according to their personal judgment and convictions. Unlike later Liberal and Radical theories, it assumed that representation was of corporate bodies rather than individuals, and on the whole such interests were either of a local or functional nature.

The franchise reforms of 1832, 1867 and 1884 did not substantially alter the dominance of men with independent means. Redlich observed in 1908 that, although one would expect a broader suffrage to result in the incorporation of numerous classes into the legislative body,

> . . . a glance at the actual conditions in present day parliaments will, even on casual inspection, reveal that nowhere has this consequence followed to the extent that might have been expected . . . Participation in parliamentary life calls for a total or partial abandonment of the work of earning a livelihood and thus a substantial advantage falls to the share of the higher and financially independent classes.[9]

He cites figures from *Dod's Parliamentary Companion* to show that among the 670 Members of the House of Commons in 1904 were to be found: 119 lawyers, 77 large manufacturers, 11 railway directors, 22 shipowners and marine engineers, 29 bankers and stockbrokers, 12 mine owners, 52 merchants, 18 newspaper editors and proprietors, 15 journalists, 6 doctors, 7 authors, 7 professors and schoolmasters, 54 military and naval men, 10 former diplomatists and civil servants, 26 landed proprietors and 47 country gentlemen.

The dominance of landed interests waned during the nineteenth century, but outside interests such as inherited or acquired wealth, or at least membership of a profession such as law, which could be combined with legislative duties, were still necessary. Additionally, the rise of the limited liability company provided the House with a new species of part-time legislators, who were also part-time directors in commerce and industry. Echoing Bagehot's observations on England as a deferential nation, Redlich attributes the persistence of the historic structure of the House of Commons not just to financial considerations such as the high cost of elections and the non-payment of Members, but also to the fact that the electorate preferred to give its votes to leaders of society. Precisely because of its emphasis on independence, the rise of Liberal theory in the nineteenth century also helped to preserve a continuing acceptance of the tradition of the financially independent Member with outside interests or employment. In the absence of receiving an official salary MPs had to have independent incomes.

All of this is not to infer that the non-payment of Members and the consequent financial circumstances and practices of MPs during the eighteenth and nineteenth centuries went unchallenged. As early as 1780 payment of Members was advocated by a committee set up by the Westminster electors and this demand was taken up by the Society for Constitutional Reform. It was also incorporated in a Reform Bill of 1830, figured as one of the six political demands in the People's Charter drawn up in 1838, and in the late nineteenth century was campaigned for by reforming organisations such as the National Democratic League, and the Metropolitan Radical Federation. It also became a priority of the Labour Party in their struggle in the early twentieth century to get representatives into Parliament. Despite this agitation, and a string of motions or Bills supporting payment which were brought before the House of Commons in 1870, 1888, 1892, 1893, 1895 and 1903, membership of Parliament remained an unpaid occupation until 1912. In the preceding year the House agreed by 256 votes to 158 to accept a motion introduced by the Liberal Government for MPs to be entitled to draw £400 per annum from public funds (*Parl Debs* 29:1911, 1365–1484).

Mr. Lloyd George, the Chancellor of the Exchequer, defended the motion for payment on the grounds that parliamentary work and conditions had changed since the nineteenth century and Members could no longer consider Parliament as an adjunct to a business or professional career. The provision would allow those to enter Parliament whose limited means would otherwise prevent their taking up a political career. The Liberal Government had only narrowly won the two 1910 General Elections and had quickly become dependent on Labour and Irish Nationalist support to maintain its parliamentary majority. The measure was largely a response to Labour Party pressure following the Osborne Judgement of 1909, which had declared illegal the use of the Trade Union levy to finance Members, and was designed in particular to help Labour MPs whose jobs could hardly be combined with service in the House of Commons. By establishing a public allowance for MPs, it rescued the Labour Party from the expense of paying each of its MPs £200 a year out of its parliamentary fund.

Though willing to concede the necessity for remuneration of MPs out of public funds, the Liberal Government insisted that a commercial standard for payment was inappropriate in the public service. In their philosophy a public servant should be made an allowance 'to enable him to maintain himself comfortably and honourably, but not luxuriously, during the time he is rendering service to the State' (*Parl Debs* 29: 1911, 1382). The proposed payment to Members was just such a minimum allowance. It was not a recognition of the magnitude of service, nor was it provided to enable a Member to meet the expenses of his parliamentary duties as the current usage of 'parliamentary allowances' infers. This modest aim did not appease Conservative Members who opposed the Motion primarily on the grounds that it violated the principle of gratuitous public service and would lead to the extinction of the independent, part-time Member. They feared the advent of a full-time House of Commons, composed entirely of professional politicians with no business connections of any kind, and were suspicious that this was the intention of Mr. Lloyd George's policy. Supporters of the measure, on the other hand, could not understand how its opponents could make out that 'it would tend more to the dignity of the House that Members should be dependent for their salaries on outside organisations representing sectional interests rather than on the taxes of the nation' (*Parl Debs* 29:1911, 1475).

Four days later the House, in Committee, approved a motion to grant a sum not exceeding £252,000, to His Majesty to defray the charge incurred by Members' salaries (*Parl Debs* 29:1911, 1579–1682). The Opposition challenged the constitutionality of this procedure, which they argued provided a sum of money for initiating a new policy by means of Resolution and Vote and not by Act of Parliament. The matter gained significance because the House of Commons had only just passed the Parliament Act, depriving the Lords of the right to deal with financial questions, and now they risked the charge of impropriety in voting salaries to themselves.

An Opposition Member seized on this apparent conflict of interest in Members voting on their own salaries and sought to test the rule of the House regarding voting with a pecuniary interest (see page 41) by moving a motion to disallow a vote. The chairman had anticipated this question and, having regard to precedent, he judged that in this case Members did have a private and pecuniary interest, but that they also had an overriding public and general interest. Thus he refused leave for the motion to disallow a vote to be put to the Committee.

Payment of Members – A Break with Tradition?

The tradition of part-time service and the presumption of outside interests did not die with the introduction of official payment. Until the Boyle Report in 1971 which recommended MPs should be paid on a full-time basis, the extent of the parliamentary allowance was largely influenced by two factors. Firstly, many Members continued to believe membership was, and should be, part-time. Secondly, allied with this, many MPs still possessed outside sources of income, either in the traditional forms discussed above, or increasingly through business affiliations (directorships, shareholdings etc), or as paid advisors and consultants to a burgeoning number of interest groups and organisations. Moreover, with the growth in the number of Labour MPs elected to Parliament, there also emerged a new species of 'interested' MP – the trade-union sponsored Member, backed financially by a trade union or co-operative society. Technically all Labour candidates and therefore all Labour MPs have to have their candidature supported by one of the organisations affiliated to the Labour Party, but common usage restricts the term 'sponsored MP' to trade-union supported Members. Writing about this phenomenon in the early 1940s, the political commentator J.F.S. Ross observed that in 1937 exactly half of Labour MPs – 80 out of 160 – were backed by specific trade unions and nine were backed by co-operative societies. While acknowledging that the low level of official payment meant that dependency on trade union funding was the only way that the Labour Party could secure a reasonable share of parliamentary representation, he drew attention to the danger of sponsored MPs being obliged to represent or serve sectional interests in the House.[10]

These prevailing assumptions of part-time service and outside interests were continually buttressed by recommendations and opinions of successive Select Committee on Expenses reports. For example, the 1946 Select Committee on Members' Expenses (*HC* 93: 1954–6) did not regard the sum paid to a Member as a professional salary and felt it was unwise to curtail his freedom by paying him an amount which would demand his full-time attendance. In 1946 the salary was increased from £600 to £1,000, and salaries of £500 were introduced for MPs who, as Ministers or Leaders of the Opposition received an official salary below £5,000. MPs were also granted free travel between their homes and Westminster; free travel between Westminster and their constituencies had existed since 1924.

A similar Committee in 1954 (*HC* 72: 1954) noted the increasing difficulty of combining outside work with membership but pointed out 'some Members can, however, add to their income by directorships, by journalistic work, broadcasting, lecturing, consultative work, advising and similar tasks, which do not call for long absences from the House, and some are in receipt of payments made to them as officials of organisations'. The last part of this statement referred primarily to trade-union sponsored Labour MPs.

A third and fundamental factor determining the level of parliamentary remuneration was, of course, the crucial one of Executive influence. As Peter Richards remarks, 'Parliament is in the hands of the Executive down to such details as its own pay and allowances'.[11] Any proposed increase in Members' salary represents a value judgment of what *is* an appropriate salary for a Member and, particularly in times of economic difficulties and restraint, Governments have not been prepared to risk 'public' outrage by raising MPs' salaries. What is, therefore, already a sensitive issue is made all the more so by the fact that Members are in the unique position of being seen to vote on their own salaries.

In reality then, prior to the implementation of the Boyle recommendations, an MP's pay was too low, relative to necessary expenditures incurred in carrying out his parliamentary duties, to ensure his proper maintenance. Aware of this, and with due regard to their long-term security, MPs were encouraged, if not forced, to acquire or retain outside interests or employment which would provide supplementary income.

The inadequacy of the official allowance was aggravated by changes both in the composition of Parliament and in its functions. In the first place the number of MPs elected to the House who relied solely on the parliamentary allowance for income increased. These were for the most part Labour MPs whose former employment was totally incompatible with membership of the House. They were typical of the growing number of MPs being elected who regarded membership not as an adjunct to a legal or business career, or as a reward for service in the Labour Movement, but as a full-time job. Secondly, as Michael Rush has identified, the expansion of government activity, and in particular the growth of the welfare state, inevitably placed more demands upon MPs.[12] Not only did the time spent in the House or in its Committees dealing with parliamentary business increase, but Members were also faced with an expanding 'welfare' role in their constituencies; all of which created further expenses to be met from an already inadequate salary.

Modest improvements were won in Members' salary and tenure conditions during the 1960s, and as we shall see in chapter 5, these coincided with the modern wave of concern over Members' outside financial interests. In 1965 the first comprehensive pensions scheme was introduced for MPs and dependents (Members' Pensions Act 1965). In 1969 three further provisions were authorised: free postage on parliamentary business; free telephone calls within the UK; and a secretarial allowance of up to £500 – an allowance not of right, but reimbursement of money spent on this particular item. Other expenses incurred in respect of parliamentary duties still had to be met from the parliamentary allowance, although these could often be claimed by the MP against income tax. The parliamentary allowance itself had risen periodically, but at the rate of £3,250 in 1970, it was still an inducement for MPs to seek remunerative outside interests and occupations in addition to their public duties.

Top Salaries Review Body: Payment of the Full-Time Member

Labour plans to set up a special panel, under the Commission for Industry and Manpower Bill, to review (amongst other public salaries) parliamentary pay, died with the 1970 General Election. The incoming Conservative Government decided instead to refer the issue of Members' pay to an independent review body, with the proviso that the ultimate decision regarding pay and allowances must remain with Parliament. In May 1971 the Top Salaries Review Body was set up under the chairmanship of Lord Boyle (since 1981, Lord Plowden) and seven months later produced its First Report on the pay and pension arrangements for Ministers and Members of Parliament (Cmnd 4836: 1971).

The Review Body grasped the importance of the fundamental

problem of choosing the basis upon which MPs' remuneration should be assessed, that is, whether their job should be treated as full-time or part-time in determining the level of pay. They believed that while the principle of payment was no longer hotly disputed as it had been in 1911, this question had never received an authoritative answer. It had been considered by the Lawrence Committee set up in 1963 to review payment to MPs and Ministers, but they had declined to express an opinion either way (Cmnd 2516:1964).

Nor was there an abundance of empirical data upon which authoritative judgments could be made. In formulating their opinion on the subject the Review Body conducted a survey of the circumstances of Members of Parliament and of their views on remuneration, and in their Report recorded that,

> Our survey . . . has shown . . . that 70 per cent of Members other than office-holders pursue some other regular or occasional occupation; though in many cases the amount of time spent on the other occupation is quite small. Nearly 60 per cent of the Members concerned spend under 10 hours per week pursuing their other occupations while Parliament is sitting, and a further 29 per cent spend from 10 to 19 hours per week. Two-thirds of these Members earn over £1,000 per year from their other occupations, over one-third more than £3,000, and one-fifth earn over £5,000, with the higher figures tending to be earned by Members with constituencies in or near London. As is to be expected, Members with other occupations spend less time both in attending the House and on other Parliamentary business. We found that involvement in an outside occupation was regarded by at least three out of four Members as beneficial to the work of Parliament by keeping Members in touch with other areas of life and providing expertise helpful to the work of Parliament. Only a small number of those pursuing other occupations felt that it was a disadvantage which was forced on them by financial necessity. Many Members, however, have been at pains to point out to us that the job of an MP is increasingly becoming full-time and that it becomes progressively more difficult to combine it satisfactorily with another regular occupation. (Cmnd 4836:1971, para 10)

To this they added that while some three-quarters of Members considered the existing degree of involvement in other occupations was beneficial to the House, most Members felt that the salary should be assessed on a full-time basis. They estimated that only one out of 16 Members spent, or admitted to spending, less than 40 hours per week on parliamentary work, while the average for all Members included in the survey was, or was claimed to be, 63 hours (para 25). The facts disclosed in this Report about the extent of Members' outside activities added fuel to the demand for full and compulsory disclosure of Members' outside interests and remuneration.

On the basis of their survey the Review Body concluded that the present century has seen a change in the role of Members of Parliament, both in terms of what their constituents expect of them and in terms of the way in which that role is viewed by Members themselves. They recommended that:

> One effect of these changes is that the job of an MP has become increasingly full-time, and in our view it is essential that the level of remuneration should be adequate to provide for full-time Members without other sources of income. We consider that the minimum figure to which the salary of Members should forthwith be raised is £4,500. (para 36)

The Boyle Report was a landmark in the history of Members' pay not only because it determined that MPs should be paid on a full-time basis, but also because it established an important distinction between what should be paid to a Member as pure salary, and his parliamentary expenses. The recommended increase in MPs' pay to £4,500 was implemented in January 1972, as were the recommendations to raise the secretarial allowance to £1,000, to introduce an allowance of up to £750 for additional costs involved in living away from home (for example, to reimburse the cost of accommodation either near the MP's constituency or Westminster) and to provide a London supplement of £175 per annum for London MPs. Travel allowances were also extended and severance pay, amounting to three months' salary, was authorised for MPs who lost their seat at a General Election.

Ironically the distinction between salaries and expenses facilitated by the Boyle Report was to prove useful to successive Governments in their attempts to contain MPs' salaries, particularly during periods of economic stringency. It became feasible to increase the allowances to offset the burden of parliamentary expenses, while at the same time being seen to keep a tight rein on the level of official pay. As a result, between 1972 and 1982 allowances increased at a much greater rate relative to income. The Top Salaries Review Body reported at frequent intervals, but their recommendations on pay were often not implemented in full by the Government of the day. The increase to £8,000 recommended by the Review Body in 1975 was restricted by the Government to £5,750 and throughout 1975–1979 increases had to be in line with the Labour Government's incomes policy. The recommended increase in 1979 to £12,000 was phased in over three years.

Following the recommendations of the 1982 Select Committee on Members' Salaries (*HC* 208: 1982) that the Review Body on Top

Salaries should, where possible, review MPs' pay in the fourth year of every Parliament, in May 1983 it recommended a substantial increase of almost 31 per cent to bring MPs' salaries up to £19,000 per annum (Cmnd 8881). Inevitably this proved politically unacceptable to a Conservative Government concerned with cutting back public expenditure. Instead, the Government proposed a figure of £15,090, an increase of only 4 per cent. On 19 July 1983 the House rejected this proposal and voted instead for an immediate rise of 5.5 per cent to £15,308, with annual increments over five years to bring the total to £18,500 on 1 January 1987; an overall increase of 27½ per cent (*HC Debs* 46:1983, 267–352).

In addition to this substantial jump in pay, Members now enjoy a wider range of allowances: in particular, improved office, secretarial and research allowances (£11,364 for the year ending March 1984, and £12,000 for any subsequent year); improved travel concessions on parliamentary business and travel facilities for spouses and children; and increases both in the London supplement (£873) and the allowances for the additional costs of living away from their main residence (increased to £6,696 p.a. from 1 August 1984).

Pension arrangements and severance pay to offset the insecurity of office have also been revised. The Parliamentary Pensions Act, 1978 modified earlier Acts in 1965 and 1976 to provide for ill-health, retirement pensions and for increased benefits for widows and widowers of MPs. Membership of this contributory pension scheme is compulsory. The rate of accrual has changed periodically and currently stands at one-sixtieth of the pensionable salary for each year of pensionable service, with the option of purchasing added years (April 1984). However, in July 1983 MPs agreed a resolution which, with amending legislation, will increase their pension contribution rate from 6 per cent to 9 per cent of their salary, and change the rate of accrual to one-fiftieth. Pension is payable at age 65, but an early retirement option is available from age 50 onwards on an actuarially reduced pension, and MPs with 25 years' service and aged 62 can retire at a dissolution with the full accrued pension.[13]

Since 1972, MPs unseated through electoral defeat have been entitled to a terminal grant amounting to three months' salary, and in April 1975 they also became entitled to draw unemployment benefit. In 1980 the Review Body recommended that severance pay for MPs who lost their seats either through electoral defeat or through changes in constituency boundaries should be increased for MPs aged 50 or more who had completed at least 10 years' service (Report No. 13, February 1980, para 62). This proposal was modified by the House and severance pay (renamed resettlement grant) is now calculated as a percentage of annual salary rather than an amount equivalent to three or six months' salary. The resettlement grant applies to any Member who has taken the oath and varies according to age and length of service. For example, a Member aged 50 or below and with less than 10 years' service would receive a grant of 50 per cent of his annual salary if he lost his seat, whereas a Member aged between 55 and 64 with a record of at least 15 years' service is entitled to a maximum of a year's pay. At any future general election any Member over 65 who loses their seat will not receive a resettlement grant, but will instead go on to a pension.

Members' Pay: 'Uncomfortable, Embarrassing, Annual Debates'

Although the Top Salaries Review Body established the principle that MPs should be paid on a full-time basis, without the need for other sources of income, the issue of MPs' salaries has continued to be the subject of 'uncomfortable, embarrassing, annual debates' (*HC Debs* 46: 1983, 274).

In addition to the fact of MPs voting for their own salary increases, the reasons for this are largely twofold. Firstly, despite the Review Body's opinion, MPs themselves are not unanimously agreed that membership should be full-time, and in any case, they have different views on what full-time membership actually means. In practice the distinction between full-time and part-time membership is not as clear as the concepts infer. My conversations with British MPs revealed a fundamental difference of opinion between those Members who interpreted full-time membership as meaning absolutely no outside interests, and those who believed they could be full-time in terms of hours and still pursue outside interests, which are counted as 'overtime'. Attempts to restrict the full payment of any increase in pay to those MPs not receiving outside remuneration has been consistently rejected by the House. Secondly, even if payment is to be calculated on a full-time basis, this does not necessarily suggest a self-evident salary level.

The latest debate on MPs' salaries in July 1983 illustrated these problems. Contrasting the Government's proposal for £15,090 per annum with the Review Body's recommended £19,000, the Leader of the House admitted that the Government's proposed increase represented

> . . . a value judgment of what is an appropriate salary for a Member. We are all constrained to make a value judgment of what that figure should be. The TSRB report suggests that it should pay regard to a Member being full-time with no other source of income. It must also take account of the unique nature of a Member's occupation. These factors alone, however, do not indicate a self-evident salary. We have still to make our own

political judgment about an issue sensitive in its economic and social consequences. (*HC Debs* 46:1983, 273)

The difficult position of the Leader of the House on these occasions of debating MPs' pay should not be overlooked. He has to consider the best interests of the House, while also having an allegiance to party and Government. It is all too easy, as in this debate, to risk the accusation of sacrificing the interests of the House to party loyalty, or more specifically to a temporary political ambition of that particular party.

Disagreements about MPs' pay also go deeper than differences of opinion on the appropriate 'rate for the job'. A small number of MPs, the most vociferous being Mr. Enoch Powell, go so far as to dispute even the principle of evaluating in money terms the abilities of MPs, their services and their labours. For them the salary is essentially an arbitrary or nominal figure. As was the case prior to 1911, membership is exalted as a privilege which requires some sort of sacrifice, even to the extent of doing the job for nothing.

It has often been suggested that these 'uncomfortable, embarrassing, annual debates' on MPs' pay could be avoided by linking it to that of an analogous outside group or groups; most commonly with the rank of Assistant Secretary in the Civil Service. Such proposals have in the past failed for various reasons, not least because successive Governments have thought it politically damaging to remove from the House the responsibility of settling MPs' pay directly in the light of prevailing circumstances, and to subject it instead to automatic adjustments. Nevertheless, during the July 1983 backbench revolt on Members' pay, MPs voted to accept a resolution to link MPs' pay from 1 January 1988 to the salary paid to a civil servant at a point in the grade of national salaries receiving £18,500 on 13 June 1983 (*HC Debs* 46:1983, 267–352).

It is unclear which grade in the Civil Service this refers to, but it is not the rank of Assistant Secretary as previously suggested.[14] Members' pay has nevertheless been fixed for the next five years and with this move it would seem that, subject to any further resolution by the House, the recommendation by the Select Committee on Members' Salaries in 1982 that Parliament should review MPs' pay in the fourth year of each Parliament with a view to setting the rate for the next Parliament, has been suspended. The extent to which linkage with the civil service grade will remove the issue of Members' salaries from the political arena remains to be seen, but as Mr. Edward Heath observed at the time of this decision, the delicate issue of Members' pay now takes on a new dimension:

> One must also consider the attitude of the Civil Service to linkage. We are asking the Civil Service to carry the House through what it finds to be an unpleasant, difficult and objectionable

business . . . If I were a permanent secretary to a Department, or if I were a union leader of a Civil Service Union, I would immediately say that any Government were bound to be affected in their treatment of the Civil Service pay by the recognition that the result would then be applied to the House of Commons. (*HC Debs* 46:1983, 315)

Implications for Conflict of Interest Restraints

In this chapter we have consistently seen the interconnection between Members' pay and allowances, and the possession of outside interests. The tradition of the financially independent Member, with the accompanying view of membership as a part-time occupation, carried with it the presumption that it was proper, and indeed before 1911 necessary, for Members to possess outside financial interests. Both tradition and presumption to a large extent survived the introduction of official payment in 1911 and, at least until the Boyle Report in 1971, were the basis for settling MPs' remuneration. As we shall see, they also formed a continuing thread underlying the development of rules and conventions regulating Members' pecuniary interests. The propriety of Members' possessing outside interests has never been questioned by the House, simply the means by which some of these should be disclosed.

A change in the philosophy of payment of Members occurred with the Boyle Committee's recommendation that the level of remuneration should be adequate to provide for full-time Members without other sources of income. However, we have discovered that this does not suggest a self-evident salary level, nor does it mean that Members will automatically discard outside interests and employment. My sample survey of Members indicates that over two-thirds of the House which approved the Register still believed that MPs should be able to have outside interests, and that a similar proportion actually had outside paid or unpaid employment.[15] Many MPs believe that they can be full-time in terms of hours spent in the House or its Committees or on constituency work and still have the energy to pursue outside interests as 'overtime'.

Members interviewed in my sample survey were asked whether they in fact agreed that MPs should be paid on a full-time basis. Although 77 per cent believed they should, well over half of these Members added the proviso that MPs should nevertheless be able to retain and seek outside financial interests and employment. Less than one-third of the sample, all Labour MPs who had voted for the Register, insisted that MPs should be regarded as full-time with no outside financial interests and correspondingly paid an 'adequate' salary. Inevitably the sample indicated disagreement among parliamentarians as to what would constitute an 'adequate' parliamentary salary. Giving their views on the then current salary level (£9,450) only one-third of the sample said it was adequate, just under two-thirds said it was inadequate but improving, while two senior Conservative MPs condemned it as inadequate and unlikely ever to become adequate.

When asked directly whether it would be feasible, and indeed desirable, to reduce the risk of real or apparent conflict of interest by raising salaries further and banning outside interests and employment altogether, only 13 per cent of the sample thought it would be *both* feasible *and* desirable (a further 10 per cent throught it would be desirable but not feasible). The most common objections raised by Members were that such a move would erode the independence of MPs and deprive the House of valuable experience and expertise. The overwhelming impression gained was that such a proposal for reform – a reversal of the situation prior to 1911 – would be an anathema to a body which has traditionally supported the practice of the financially independent Member and has seen fit to impose very few restrictions on their outside interests and employment.

4 The Tradition of the Honourable Member

While Parliament has traditionally promoted the role of the financially independent Member, a consequence is that it has adopted a far less interventionist role in ensuring a Member's disassociation from his personal interests. In this chapter we shall explore this assertion and trace the vague anthology of rules and conventions which emerged to regulate Members' private financial interests prior to the adoption of the Register of Members' interests in 1974.

The individual Member has long been regarded the best judge in avoiding conflict situations. In contrast to the detailed code drawn up for Ministers, Parliament has provided no coherent code to guide Members' conduct in the area of pecuniary interests. Instead there has grown up little by little a vague anthology of resolutions, Speaker's rulings, recommendations from committees of privilege, traditional conventions and so on, which are intended as a guide to Members in exercising their discretion. These may be classified as preventive regulations in that they are intended to regulate the potential harm *before* the conflict occurs. In this sense they can be distinguished from the remedial procedures involved in the investigation and punishment of misconduct, which are discussed in greater detail in chapter 6.

This distinction forms the organising principle for the ensuing factual presentation of the preventive rules, regulations and procedures governing Members' pecuniary interests prior to the introduction of the Register. Inevitably there is some overlap between the two areas. This derives largely from the fact that the history of the regulation of Members' conduct is interlinked with the history of parliamentary privilege, which not only provides the standards to be observed in parliamentary proceedings, but also affords Parliament the right to regulate and, if necessary, punish the conduct of Members who abuse its privileges.

Parliamentary Privilege

The privilege of freedom of speech is central to the issue of conflict of interest. First claimed in 1541, and ultimately given statutory recognition in 1689 in article 9 of the Bill of Rights this states, 'That the freedom of speech, and debates or proceedings in Parliament, ought not to be impeached or questioned in any court or place out of Parliament'.

This provision has at least two implications for the regulation of Members' financial interests. Firstly, it protects the freedom of speech in Parliament and places a corollary duty on each Member to refrain from any course of action prejudicial to the privilege which he enjoys; a principle underlying many of the preventive rules in the area of pecuniary interests. Secondly, it conveys recognition of the sole right of each House itself to adjudicate upon the conduct of its Members *in their parliamentary capacity*, a right reaffirmed by a resolution of the House in 1837 (*CJ* [1837] 418–419). The claim to this right in part derives from the historical origins of Parliament as the High Court of Parliament, the highest court in the land, and the conception that it would therefore be contrary to every principle for its proceedings to be regulated or challenged in any other court.

Parliamentary privilege rests on the law and custom of Parliament and is defined in Erskine May as

> . . . the sum of peculiar rights enjoyed by each House collectively as a constituent part of the High Court of Parliament, and by each House individually, without which they could not discharge their functions, and which exceed those possessed by other bodies or individuals. Thus privilege though part of the law of the land, is to a certain extent one exemption from the ordinary law.[1]

The privileges of the House of Commons with which we are primarily concerned are

> The sum of the fundamental rights of the House and of its individual Members as against the prerogatives of the Crown, the authority of the ordinary courts of law and the special rights of the House of Lords.[2]

The practice of claiming these rights – which include freedom from arrest and legal process, freedom of speech, debate and proceedings in the House, freedom from intimidation or molestation (including bribes or financial inducements), freedom to punish as contempt breaches of privilege under the foregoing headings and an indeterminate class of obstructions and indirect interference whether by speech, action or writing[3] – can be traced back at least to the fifteenth century, if not further. The distinctive mark of privilege is its *ancillary* character. The privileges claimed by Parliament are those which are 'absolutely necessary for the due execution of its powers' (*Erskine May*, 19 ed.) and such rights and immunities are enjoyed by individual members *only* as a means to ensure the effective discharge of the functions of the House.

Without the power to enforce compliance with its commands, to punish offenders and to discipline its own Members, the privileges of Parliament would be ineffectual in ensuring its efficient functioning and dignity. Thus, when

> . . . any of these rights and immunities, both of the Members, individually, and of the assembly in its collective capacity, which are known by the general name of privileges, are disregarded or attacked by any individual or authority, the offence is called breach of privilege, and is punishable under the law of Parliament. Each House also claims the right to punish actions, which, while not breaches of any specific privilege, are offences against its authority or dignity . . . any such actions, though often called 'breaches of privilege' are more properly distinguished as 'contempts'.[4]

There is no formal codification in this area and Parliament emphasises the advantages to be gained from the indefinite and discretionary nature of the law of Parliament. Sir Barnett Cocks, a former Clerk of the House, explained to the Committee of Privileges in 1964 that

> The reason for keeping the privilege of Parliament undefined has been stressed in the Report of the Select Committee on the Official Secrets Act, in its report of 5 April 1939. They say: 'The privileges of Parliament, like many other institutions of the British Constitution, are indefinite in their nature and stated in general and sometimes vague terms. The elasticity thus secured has made it possible to apply existing privileges in new circumstances from time to time. Any attempt to translate them into precise rules must deprive them of the very quality which renders them adaptable to new and varying conditions, and new or unusual combinations of circumstances, and indeed might have the effect of restricting rather than safeguarding Members' privileges.' (*HC* 247: 1964, para 239)

Preventive Regulations

It would be an enormous task to enumerate every Act, resolution, Speaker's ruling, etc. which has contributed incrementally to the anthology of preventive regulations governing Members' pecuniary interests. Bearing in mind these are designed to uphold the general freedoms and obligations deriving from parliamentary privilege in the specific area of Members' interests, it is sufficient to outline, and in some cases illustrate, the landmarks in the nature and development of these scattered rules.

We shall follow the approach of the 1969 Select Committee on Members' Interests (Declaration) (*HC* 57: 1969) by considering the factual position of these rules, conventions etc. in terms of three elements: the statutory requirements and resolutions of the House governing the offering to and acceptance by Members of payments or rewards; the rules governing voting with a pecuniary interest; and the custom requiring a declaration of interest. In addition to this loose collection of rules and conventions, it should be pointed out that Members' power to confer direct financial benefit on their constituents or other individuals or groups is constitutionally limited. The House's standing order no. 82, established more than 250 years ago, provides that no motion for a grant or charge upon the public revenue is to be proceeded with unless recommended by the Crown. As the 1969 Select Committee observed 'Ministers subject to their own strict rules of conduct and a civil service bred in a tradition of impartiality and incorruptibility dispose of that recommendation' (*HC* 57: 1969, para 87).

Payments and rewards to Members

Restrictions on a Member's freedom to take up outside paid employment are few, and operate only when his outside interests influence the discharge of his duties as a Member.

In 1782 when the belief that MPs should be independent of royal influence was widely held, an Act was passed to exclude government contractors from the House of Commons (22 George III, c.45). By the middle of the nineteenth century with the progress of industrialisation, particularly the growth of incorporated enterprises, this Act had become an anachronism. The law on disqualification for membership of the House of Commons through holding certain posts, including ministerial and other offices under the Crown, remained exceedingly complicated until the passing of the House of Commons Disqualification Act, 1957 (later re-enacted as the House of Commons Disqualification Act, 1975). This replaced a large number of statutory and common law provisions on disqualification by a single code, and also repealed the existing legislation disqualifying a Member on his becoming a public contractor. In recommending the latter deletion, the Select Committee which considered the bill in 1955–56 argued that the existing law was archaic and that there had been no knowledge of corruption affecting Members in connection with government contracts for the past hundred years. They did however stress that the repeal of this provision would emphasise the obligation on Members to disclose any pecuniary interest when speaking or voting (see below).

Another disqualification for membership which stems from payment of Members is corrupt practices at elections. This is dealt with by the provisions now contained in subsections 139 and 140 of the Representation of the People Act of 1949.

In addition to these statutory restrictions, the House has formally condemned the offering to and acceptance by Members of bribes. Following the findings of an enquiry that some Members of the House of Commons had been bribed in connection with matters concerning East India trade, the House resolved on 2 May 1695 that:

> The offer of money, or other advantage, to a Member of Parliament for the promoting of any matter whatsoever, depending or to be transacted in Parliament is a high crime and misdemeanour and tends to the subversion of the English Constitution. (*CJ* [1693–97] 331)

In the spirit of this resolution the House has regarded the offering of a bribe to a Member of either House in order to influence him in his conduct as a Member, or of any 'fee or reward in connection with the promotion of or opposition to any bill, resolution, matter or thing submitted to the House or a Committee thereof', as a breach of privilege (*Erskine May*, 19 ed. p 149).

However, as pointed out by Geoffrey Marshall, more recently 'alleged financial impropriety has not invariably been a matter of straight forward bribery, but turned upon the relationships between Members and special interest groups or their representatives'.[5] Here a considerable degree of uncertainty still remains. The House had traditionally attempted to draw a distinction between illicit forms of payment on the one hand, and on the other, financial assistance from outside bodies – such as trade unions, public quoted companies etc. – the payment and receipt of which does not in itself involve any breach of privilege. However, difficulties can arise from the latter form of financial relationship if the sponsoring body withdraws or threatens withdrawal of assistance on account of the Member's activities in Parliament, and thereby risks the accusation of fettering the complete independence of the Member. Following the Committee of Privilege's investigation of the case of Mr. W.J. Brown MP and the Civil Service Clerical Association in 1947 (*HC* 118: 1947), the House attempted to clarify its position by resolving that,

> It is inconsistent with the dignity of the House, with the duty of a Member to his constituents, and with the maintenance of the privilege of freedom of speech, for any Member of this House to enter into any contractual agreement with an outside body, controlling or limiting the Member's complete independence and freedom of action in Parliament or stipulating that he shall act in any way as the representative of such outside body in regard to any matters to be transacted in Parliament; the duty of a Member being to his constituents and to the country as a whole, rather than to any particular section thereof. (*CJ* [1946–47] 310)

However, this resolution, based on one of two principles governing Members' relationships with outside bodies set out in the Committee's report, is difficult to reconcile with the other principle expressed by the Committee and endorsed by the House. The second principle acknowledged the fact that many Members do receive financial assistance from outside bodies, and that not every action by an outside body that may influence the conduct of a Member can be regarded as a breach of privilege, *even* if it were calculated and intended to bring pressure on a Member to take or refrain from taking a course of action.

In addition to safeguarding against pecuniary corruption arising from direct payments to Members, the House has sought to guard against indirect influence by forbidding Members to accept fees for professional services connected with proceedings in Parliament. Members may not practise as counsel before the House or any of its committees; nor may they advise, as counsel, on a private bill or parliamentary proceeding. These principles concerning professional advocacy have been formally recognised in several resolutions of the House.

On 6 November 1666 the House resolved:

> That such Members of this House are of the long robe shall not be counsel on either side, in any bill depending in the Lords' House, before such bill shall come down from the Lords' House to this House. (*CJ* [1660–67] 646)

It was declared on similar grounds in 1830 that it was contrary to the law and usage of Parliament for any Member to be engaged, either by himself or any partner, in the management of private bills before either House of Parliament for pecuniary reward (*CJ* [1830] 107). Again on 22 June 1858 the House ordered:

> That it is contrary to the usage and derogatory to the dignity of this House that any of its Members should bring forward, promote or advocate in this House any proceeding or measure in which he may have acted or been concerned for or in consideration of any pecuniary fee or reward. (*CJ* [1857–58] 247)

These prohibitions against professional advocacy arose during the centuries when private legislation of a local, sectional or personal nature comprised the vast bulk of the business of the House. The 1660 resolution very obviously relates to members of the legal profession, and the 1858 resolution, though couched in broad terms, was similarly agreed by the House in the context of advocacy by members of the bar.

Voting with a pecuniary interest

> . . . a personal interest in a question disqualified a Member from voting. But this interest, it should be further understood, must be a direct pecuniary interest, and separately belonging to the persons whose votes were questioned, and not in common with the rest of his Majesty's subjects, or on a matter of State policy. (*Parl Debs* 20:1811, 1000–1012)

In response to a motion for the disallowing of votes of certain Members on the Gold Coin Bill in 1811, Speaker Abbot gave this oft-quoted interpretation of the House rule, established since at least the seventeenth century, regarding voting with a pecuniary interest. His ruling expressed significant qualifications to the fundamental principle that no Member with a direct pecuniary interest in a question may be allowed to vote on it, and these qualifications have been further defined by later Speakers. A 'direct pecuniary interest' to be covered by the ruling must be private and particular and not dependent on the possible exercise of permissive powers by another body.

In the evidence to the 1969 Select Committee on Members' Interests (Declaration) the Clerk of the House of Commons clarified this point by referring to the Local Taxation, Customs and Excise Duties Bill, 1890, which granted compensation for public house licences which were to be extinguished. Three MPs – all owners of public houses – voted in a division on that bill, but the Speaker ruled the motion to disallow their votes not in order because the compensation to be granted under the bill was not automatic but contingent on County Councils exercising permissive powers (*HC* 57: 1969, Evidence Q 1).

Further, 'not in common with the rest of His Majesty's subjects' has meant that membership of a category or group which stands to benefit has not precluded a Member from voting. For example, as we have discovered, Members are entitled to vote on the question of their own salaries, and a farmer or industrialist may vote on measures benefiting the industry in which he is engaged. If the expected benefit is public or general, the personal private gain by the individual Member is incidental (*Parl Debs* 29:1911, 1681–2)

Linked to this criterion, the inclusion of the words 'or on a matter of State policy' explain the difference in treatment by the House of questions of a personal interest in respectively private bills and public bills. If the interest is on a matter of State policy, whether the question involves the pecuniary interest of all members of the community or only certain groups, the benefit is held to be general and therefore not disallowable. Thus neither directors nor shareholders in public companies are excluded from voting for or against a public bill which might regulate that company, even if it is one particular company about which the bill is concerned. Votes on private bills, which are not matters of State policy, are not covered by this proviso.

In 1896 the question of whether it was desirable to define more precisely the nature and extent of personal and pecuniary interest which should disable a Member from voting was remitted to a select committee of the House. This followed the second reading of the London and North-Western Railway Bill, where Mr. Lloyd-George had moved to disallow the vote of a Tory Member on the grounds of personal pecuniary interest in the Bill. The Member was a director of the company.

The 1896 Select Committee on Members of Parliament (Personal Interest) concluded that a more precise definition of interest could only be arrived at and maintained by the enactment of a standing order, and that they could not recommend this because

> . . . No Standing Order could include all the possible varieties, present or prospective, of personal pecuniary interest, and any Standing Order must necessarily be both strictly and narrowly interpreted by the Speaker or the Chairman. The enactment of a Standing Order might, therefore, actually facilitate such arrangements by any Members who might desire to make an improper use of their votes as would enable them to do so with impunity; while the very uncertainty and width of the present definition, which admits of infinite degrees of variation, according to the judgment of the House on the merits of each individual case would deter them from any attempt of this kind. (*HC* 274: 1896, p. iv)

The Committee did not respond to the suggested amendment to the standing order relating to private bills (contained in an appendix by Mr. F.B. Palmer, Barrister at Law), the acceptance of which would have precluded a director of a company from voting in Parliament on affairs of that company. It has been argued that this refusal by the Committee to accept tighter restrictions upon MPs who were directors left the way open to MPs being directly subsidised by trade union funds:

> The refusal to impose new restrictions upon private Members' interests in 1896, when the influence of business on politics appeared dangerous to the public interest, left no logical ground for restrictions upon the interest of organized Labour in the

> future. The rise of the Labour Party with many of its candidates subsidized by union funds clearly raised the question of interest. But if it had been all right for business corporations to have direct representation, on what grounds could even a whole party of Trade Union representatives be restricted.[6]

The effect of the various rulings since Speaker Abbot's ruling in 1811 is that on a *public bill* there is no obligation for a Member to refrain from voting. Since that time there has only been one recorded instance of votes on a public matter being disallowed, when in 1892 on a motion for a grant in aid of a survey for a projected East African railway the votes of three Members who were directors or shareholders in the British East Africa Company were disallowed (*CJ* [1892] 98). There is no record of a vote being disallowed on a public bill.

However, the position is different with regard to private legislation. The promoters of a private bill are seeking special rights or powers and therefore cannot be said to be 'in common with the rest of His Majesty's subjects', nor is their bill 'a matter of State policy'. Nevertheless, even on a private bill the interest which would disable a Member from voting would have to be a very direct personal interest and not just of a local nature. In evidence to the 1969 Select Committee on Members' Interests (Declaration) the Clerk of the House illustrated this point by confirming that a Member would not be disabled from voting on a private bill such as the Brighton Marina Bill just because he lived in Brighton (*HC* 57: 1969, Evidence Q 6). The case history of votes on matters affected by personal pecuniary interest is thoroughly set out in *Erskine May* 19 ed., and it is sufficient to record here that the last occasion on which a motion to disallow a Member's vote on a private bill was moved was in 1901, and the last recorded occasion on which such a motion was carried was in 1836.

If a Member disregards the rules and votes on a matter in which he has a direct interest this would not be a breach of privilege but rather a breach of convention. The penalty resides in the motion to disallow his vote and this objection must be raised immediately after the division; if taken at a later stage the Speaker would not allow it. The same procedure applies to Standing Committees. The Speaker has to rule whether, in the circumstances of the case, the motion is in order, and if he does so, the House decides the matter. The Member whose vote is impugned is allowed to plead his defence, but must withdraw before the question is proposed. It should be noted that the rule applies only to the *vote* of an MP and does not disable him from speaking to or moving a motion in which he has a personal interest.

The disallowance of a vote on the grounds of personal interest is confined to *pecuniary* interests, although it was remarked by Speaker Gully in evidence to the 1896 Select Committee that Members

> . . . also know that it is desirable that they should abstain in some cases where their interest is not a pecuniary one, but in which the House would feel that it is better that they did not vote, and in many cases of that kind they do abstain. (*HC* 274: 1896, Q 158)

The spirit of this practice can be found in the current edition of *Erskine May*, where it is recorded that

> Disallowance of a vote on the score of personal interest is restricted to cases of pecuniary interest and has not been extended to those occasions when the dictates of self-respect and of respect due to the House might demand that a Member should refrain from taking part in a division.

It must be stressed that while pronouncements of the Chair provide guidance for Members as to what general precedents govern the practice of voting with a pecuniary interest, these do not override the primary role given to the discretion of the individual Member. Members 'individually must be the judges themselves on the question of personal interest' advised Mr. Speaker Fitzroy (*HC* 261: 1932, 192), and in 1946 Mr. Speaker Clifton Brown confirmed that:

> The question whether an Hon. Member's interest in the matter on which a Division takes place, is of such a kind that he should refrain from voting is a question of which the Member himself is, in the first instance, the judge. (*HC* 431: 1946, 1614–1616)

Declaration of interest

The only formal declaration of pecuniary interest required by a standing order of the House relates to opposed private bills. This was adopted in the mid-nineteenth century when private bill procedure, particularly that concerning railway activities, was at a peak. As we have seen, prior to 1844 Members were allotted to private bill committees specifically because of their local or personal interest in the issue, the rationale behind this system being that

> . . . the Members best qualified to serve on the committee . . . were those who had some personal, local, or professional knowledge of the matter, and who represented interests likely to be affected.[7]

Growing opinion that the dangers of vested interests more than counterbalanced the advantages to be gained from local or personal knowledge, as well as the growth in public companies and volume of public business, which rendered the 1782 reforms an anachronism led to a reform in private bill procedure. In 1848 Gladstone required a declaration of disinterestedness, local and personal, from Members serving on railway bill committees, and in 1855 this principle of impartiality was required of members of committees hearing any opposed private bills. The declaration which Members have to sign before attending and voting on a committee on an opposed private bill is now under standing order 120 (Private business).

In examination by the 1896 Select Committee on Members' Interests Speaker Gully was asked whether the rule for private bill committees should be extended to govern votes in the House. He advised that,

> I think it would be extremely inconvenient to apply that in the House; it would raise infinite questions. It is a very different thing to impose a rule of that sort on five or seven Members dealing with three or four particular matters referred to them, and to impose it on 670 Members dealing with every question that may possibly come up before the House. (*HC* 274: 1896, Q 158)

Although there are on record occasional examples during the nineteenth century of declarations of interest, the available evidence suggests that during this time personal pecuniary interest was seen mainly as raising a problem with regard to voting, rather than as necessitating a rule governing declaration in debate. However, within the House there has always been a tradition that Members should be frank in debate about their pecuniary interests and there has evolved a convention, of uncertain origin, that Members should declare their personal interest in a subject under debate. Describing this convention to the 1969 Select Committee, the Clerk of the House confirmed that this obligation is only a convention and not a rule such as a decision of the Chair or a standing order or resolution of the House:

> Erskine May only deals with the rule affecting the vote of a Member and no mention is made in the whole of this volume about speeches. This is a pretty recent convention. Again, it is a convention such as the convention of addressing Members 'hon. Member', it is not a rule which is laid down by the House; it is a convention which is observed by Members of the House. (*HC* 57: 1969, Q 13)

Various Speakers have, however, given guidance on this convention. In 1953 Mr. Speaker Morrison referred to it by stating:

> There is a custom whereby hon. Members, in making speeches, if they have an interest, declare it. I think myself that that has grown up as a matter of custom because Members desire to be frank with their fellow Members and it is sometimes a matter of prudence, in case an hon. Member should be suspected of unavowed motives. (*HC Debs* 510:1953, 2040)

Subsequent Speakers have restated Speaker Morrison's view, but have not been consistent among themselves. In 1956 the Deputy Speaker restricted the ambit of declaration to 'a direct pecuniary interest' (*HC Debs* 557:1956, 358), while in 1965 Mr. Speaker Hylton-Foster appeared to widen the criteria for interest by including shareholdings (*HC Debs* 712:1965, 525). One aspect on which successive Speakers have been consistent is the exclusion of Parliamentary Questions from the convention of declaration. In 1969 Mr. Speaker Hylton-Foster explained this omission as follows, 'For hon. Members to declare a personal interest when putting supplementary questions at Question Time regularly would eat into Question Time and slow it down' (*HC Debs* 779:1969, 1563).

Remarking on the apparent inconsistency and imprecision of statements from the Chair, the 1969 Select Committee suggested that this was because the issue has been treated as a matter of etiquette rather than a rule. This treatment has also had the effect of enshrining the assumption, promoted by the Leader of the House in 1969, that it 'has been and always must be that hon. Members can be relied upon to assess those delicate matters in an honourable and proper way and that detailed rules are undesirable and unnecessary' (*HC Debs* 783:1969, 1558).

Rules on the Private Financial Interests of Ministers

While detailed rules have been thought undesirable and unnecessary to prevent conflict of interest on the part of MPs, a contrasting approach has been taken towards Ministers. They are subject to a coherent code on private interests, in the form of written guidance issued by the Prime Minister. This code is part of a broad panopoly of measures – including the Privy Counsellor's Oath and the official secrets, copyright and public records Acts – which govern ministerial conduct. All the rules set out in the code are based on the principle that Ministers should order their affairs so that no conflict arises, or appears to arise, between their private interests and their public duties, and the onus is on individual Ministers to ensure they comply with this directive. On taking office a Minister's attention is explicitly drawn to this code and if he has any doubts about the application of the rules to his private affairs, he is urged to consult the Prime Minister, who is advised on these matters by the Secretary of the Cabinet.

The chief reason for this difference in treatment is that in contrast to general membership of Parliament, membership of the Government has been traditionally viewed as full-time employment, and a Minister is expected to devote his whole time to it. Also, as members of the

Executive, with departmental responsibilities as well as parliamentary duties, Ministers are more vulnerable than MPs to being exposed to situations where conflict of interest could arise. Unlike MPs (limited by standing order no. 82) they do have the power to recommend that a motion for a grant or charge upon public money be proceeded with, and so could confer direct financial benefit on their constituents or other individuals or groups.

Historical note

From the earliest times it has been the practice to pay for public services, and while controversy raged during the nineteenth century over the principle of paying MPs out of public funds, the question concerning Ministers was not whether they should be paid, but by what standards their salaries should be regulated in order to encourage them to put private interests on one side. Although the prevailing code of financial behaviour was, until the turn of the nineteenth century, applicable to Ministers and backbenchers alike, and even now Ministers continue to be bound by the parliamentary code of conduct, a clear distinction then emerged between the rules of behaviour concerning private financial interests applicable to the House as a whole, and those applied solely to members of the Government.

Changes in commercial practice, coupled with the financial licence of the Conservative Ministries of Salisbury and Balfour, gave rise to parliamentary agitation to regulate the holding of directorships in public companies by Ministers of the Crown. Although fuelled by the obvious contrast between the standards required from judges, civil servants, and ministers, this did not result in any noticeable changes of practice until the Liberal Government took Office in 1906. Sir Henry Campbell-Bannerman, following a principle laid down by Gladstone, ruled that 'all directorships held by Ministers must be resigned except in the case of honorary directorship in connection with philanthropic undertakings, and directorships in private companies' (*Parl Debs* 154:1906, 234). He later added that by a 'private company' he referred to one in which 'the interest of the Minister, if a director, is substantially the same as the interest of a partner in a business firm'. This rule was upheld by Mr. Stanley Baldwin in 1926, during a debate which revealed that the then Minister of Health, Mr. Neville Chamberlain, held shares in two companies which had government contracts (*HC Debs* 198: 1926, 93, 85–159). The rule was temporarily relaxed in the first National Government of 1931 (Ministers retained their directorships but did not take fees) but reaffirmed in 1935. Amendment was made in 1939 by Chamberlain who, recognising that the 1906 ruling interpreted in the modern statutory sense of 'private company' would go beyond the scope of the Campbell-Bannerman principles, announced 'private companies' in the future would apply only to those concerns 'dealing wholly or mainly with family affairs or interests and not primarily engaged in trading' (*HC Debs* 350:1939, 1937–8). He added that as this was not a rigid definition, the Prime Minister of the day must be the final judge of whether any particular directorship came within the ambit of the rule.

Sir Henry Campbell-Bannerman's ruling did not clarify the situation regarding interests such as shareholdings or speculative investments in government contracts held by Ministers. The question of shareholding arose in the Marconi affair in 1913, when three Government Ministers were rumoured to have been involved in share transactions for a profit, based on knowledge acquired in their official capacities in the Government. During debate on this affair, the Prime Minister, Mr. Asquith, doubted the wisdom of trying to lay down an exhaustive code of conduct for Ministers with regard to pecuniary matters, but set out certain rules which he felt were beyond dispute: that Ministers should not enter private transactions where a conflict of interest may arise, should not use official information for private gain and should avoid speculative investments in securities which their position and access to early or confidential information may give, or appear to give, them an advantage over others (*HC Debs* 54:1913, 556–558). These principles governing both Ministers' directorships and shareholdings were further consolidated by Winston Churchill in 1952 (*HC Debs* 496:1952, 701–703) and were reiterated by R.A. Butler on 28 January 1960, when questioned in the House about allegations that the Minister of Transport held shares in a firm contracting with the Government (*HC Debs* 616:1960, 372–3).

The rule that Ministers should not accept presents was laid down by Lord Palmerston. More recently, the danger of real or apparent conflict arising out of an obligation incurred by accepting gifts was highlighted by the Lynskey Tribunal (Cmnd 7616:1949). Mr. John Belcher, Parliamentary Secretary to the Board of Trade from January 1946 until his resignation during the course of the inquiry, was found to have received gifts and hospitality, knowing these were made for the purpose of securing favourable and expeditious treatment by the Board of Trade of applications for licences. During the debate on the tribunal's report, Winston Churchill expressed the view that utilisation of a public position for private gain cut at the root of democratic government. As Prime Minister, in 1952 he advised Ministers that it was well understood that 'no Minister or public servant should accept gifts or services which would place him under an obligation to a commercial undertaking' (*HC Debs* 496:1952, 230). This sentiment was upheld by Mr. Heath in 1973 (*HC Debs* 850:1973, 86) and again by Mrs. Thatcher in January 1980 (*HC Debs* 977:1980, 730).

Current Practice

The major features of the current written guidance to Ministers on private interests, refined and expanded from the above precedents, were set out in evidence submitted by the Cabinet Office to the Royal Commission on Standards of Conduct in Public Life (Cmnd 6524:1976, hereafter called the Salmon Commission). These were affirmed by Mrs. Thatcher in January 1983 (*HC Debs* 135:1983, 140) and can be summarised as follows:

(1) *Directorships* Ministers must on assuming office resign any directorships which they may hold, whether in public or in private companies and whether the directorship carries remuneration or is honorary. The only exception to this rule is that directorships in private companies established for the maintenance of private family estates, and only incidentally concerned in trading, may be retained; but if at any time the Minister feels that conflict is likely to arise between his private interest and his public duty, he should even in those cases divest himself of his directorship. Directorships or offices held in connection with philanthropic undertakings should also be resigned if there is any risk of conflict arising between the interests of the undertakings and the Government.

(2) *Partnerships* Ministers who are partners in professional firms, for example, solicitors, accountants, etc. should on assuming office cease to play any part in the day-to-day management of the firm's affairs. They are not necessarily required however to dissolve their partnership or allow, for example, their annual practising certificate to lapse.

(3) *Shareholdings* Ministers cannot be expected on assuming office to dispose of all their investments. But if a Minister holds a controlling interest in any company, considerations arise which are not unlike those governing the holding of directorships; and, if there is any danger of a conflict of interest, the right course is for the Minister to divest himself of his controlling interest in the company. Even where no controlling interest exists, in some instances the holding of particular shares in a concern closely connected with a Minister's own Department may give rise to the risk of a conflict of interest. Where this occurs, a Minister is advised either to divest himself of the holding, or, if appropriate, place his holding in the hands of trustees.

(4) *Investments* Ministers should avoid speculative investments in securities about which they have, or may be thought to have, early or confidential information likely to affect the price of those securities.

(5) *Underwriting* All Ministers are required on appointment to obtain permission from the Prime Minister before continuing any connection at Lloyds.

(6) *Gifts* No Minister or public servant should accept gifts or services which would place him under an obligation to a commercial undertaking.

Where a Minister does legitimately retain any private interest, there is a general rule that he should declare such an interest to his colleagues if they discuss public business in any way affecting it, and that he should dissociate himself from consideration of that business – though of course he remains fully bound by collective responsibility for such a decision. As a consequence of complying with these rules many Ministers, particularly in a Conservative Administration, are worse off financially than before taking office because they have had to give up profitable business interests.

Former Ministers This written guidance to Ministers does not extend to former Ministers taking employment or acquiring interests, such as shareholdings or directorships, on leaving office. Both Mr. MacMillan in 1962 and Mr. Wilson in 1968 refused requests from backbenchers to impose a requirement that a specified period of time should elapse between a Minister leaving office and taking up an appointment in a commercial concern with which he or his Department has had administrative associations. Nevertheless, the basic injunction that Ministers should order their affairs to prevent a conflict arising between their private interests and public duties is intended to constrain Ministers, while in office, to ensure no conflict occurs between their public duties and their foreseeable private interests on leaving office. Former Cabinet Secretary, Sir John Hunt, argued in evidence to the Salmon Commission that it would be impracticable to apply these rules to former Ministers, largely because the Government of the day would find it difficult to exercise a discretionary function in respect of Ministers of a former Aministration of a different complexion. The acceptance of this view perpetuates the discrepancy between standards applying to Ministers of the Crown and those regulating civil servants who, along with the armed forces, are the only employees in the public sector currently subject to rules about employment taken up on resignation or retirement.

Shadow Ministers Shadow Ministers are also exempt from the written guidance, and this was an issue which worried the Select Committee on Members' Conduct, set up in 1976 to inquire into the conduct and activities of MPs in connection with the Poulson affair. The Committee feared that Reginald Maudling's position as Deputy Leader of the Conservative Party (and from November 1966 until April 1968 chief Opposition spokesman on the Commonwealth, the Colonies and Overseas Development) may have led his Maltese business contacts to believe they would be 'gratifying someone who might at the time – and even more in the future (since a 'shadow' Minister is a potential future Minister) – be in a position to help Malta' (*HC* 490: 1977, para 30). While the Committee usefully highlighted the problematic position of a shadow Minister with outside interests, there is, of course, no guarantee that a future Cabinet will simply consist of shadow cabinet Ministers.

Conclusions

While Parliament has traditionally promoted the role of the financially independent Member, and jealously protected his independence from outside influences such as a corrupt electorate and undue interferences from the Crown (as manifested in the origins of parliamentary privilege) it has been far less interventionist in ensuring a Member's disassociation from his personal interests.

The fundamental question of the existence and the extent of the involvement of MPs in outside interests has rarely been considered. An exception is professional advocacy, but even here the prohibition upon accepting fees for professional services connected with proceedings in Parliament is limited to the legal profession and is therefore too narrow to cope with the modern forms of advocacy. Accordingly no backbench or frontbench Opposition Member of Parliament, in contrast to Ministers, has been prevailed upon to divest himself of those interests which may conceivably prejudice his public duties. Instead, the House has addressed itself to the question of whether, and if so how, those outside interests should be *disclosed*, and has occasionally limited the actions of Members possessing such interests, for example by restrictions on voting by Members with a pecuniary interest. Protective of the individual Member's privacy, the House has traditionally required the disclosure of interests only at the point in time of speaking or voting upon a matter upon which his action may be influenced by his personal interest. In this approach to regulating conflict of interest Parliament has therefore tended to adopt the 'principle of disclosure' in preference to the 'principle of avoidance'.[8]

The historical survey also reveals that in contrast to the detailed code which has evolved to govern Ministers' private interests, the reluctance of Parliament to intervene in the area of personal interests of Members has resulted in the lack of a codified approach towards the regulation of MPs' interests. Instead, there is an anthology of rules and conventions, developed gradually by the House and buttressed by the general principles of the law of Parliament expressed in parliamentary privilege. This pattern of development is revealing of the House's response to conflict of interest.

Firstly, the House has shown no intention of establishing, or even an awareness of any need to establish, a coherent set of rules or code of conduct, preferring instead to introduce *ad hoc* measures to clarify its position following specific instances of misconduct. This pattern of proceeding suggests that without the stimulus of periodic scandals and the resultant parliamentary and public anxiety, Parliament would not of its own accord have taken the initiative to regulate Members' interests. The history of this approach supports the premise discussed in chapter 1, that Parliament's method of proceeding in the regulating of Members' pecuniary interests has followed the course of a series of 'issue-attention' cycles.

Secondly, each act of misconduct giving rise to clarificatory rulings, resolutions etc. involved specific historical circumstances and may have occurred centuries ago. Many of the precedents which guide the Speaker and the House in their judgment on contemporary issues involving pecuniary interests are archaic and inappropriate to modern conditions. Many of the rules and conventions regulating Members' interests (particularly voting with a pecuniary interest) arose during the heyday of private bill legislation. That era has now passed, and cognisance of the changing character of legislative procedure is relevant to an evaluation of the adequacy of resolutions or Speaker's rulings formulated in the period of private legislation in the present context of predominantly public bill procedure in the House of Commons.

Thirdly, the House places great store by the flexibility of both its privileges and precedents. In a document circulated to the Cabinet during consideration of a case of alleged breach of privilege in 1947, the Attorney General advised, 'it is not necessary either to follow precedent too slavishly in this matter, or to refrain from finding that the privileges of the House are involved because there is no exact precedent in point'.[9] This apparent disregard for precedent means that even if Members look to precedent for guidance they cannot be certain that a precedent arising from a particular set of historical circumstances will necessarily be followed in similar, but inevitably not identical, circumstances at a later date. Thus the price of flexibility is uncertainty.

A consequence of the lack of a coherent code of conduct, compounded by the archaic nature and arbitrariness of precedent has been the creation of confusion among MPs as to what standards to observe in the area of pecuniary interests. Robert Boothby illustrated this point in his evidence to the Select Committee investigating his conduct:

> . . . I do want to say that I must confess I am not at all clear in my own mind about the duties of a Member of Parliament. I have sat here for 16 years, but if you ask me precisely what the duties of a Member of Parliament are with regard to disclosure, I should find it frightfully difficult to answer that question. . . . (*HC* 5: 1940–41, p 160)

The final characteristic to be identified is the unique claim of Parliament, deriving from its historical origins as the High Court of Parliament, to be the sole judge of its own proceedings, including its Members' conduct. The history of the House's regulation of conflict of interest is essentially the history of a series of loosely connected exercises in self-discipline, and as we shall discover in chapter 6 the problems associated with such regulation are essentially ones deriving from the application of self-discipline.

In using its right to exercise self-discipline to the exclusion of external sanctions the House has given primacy to the discretion of the individual Member in separating his private interests from his public duty. In doing so it has relied on the tradition of the 'honourable' Member and has emphasised the importance of individual and collective qualities such as honour, self-restraint, loyalty and mutual trust in guiding Members' judgment. The question arises as to whether these underlying values have persisted in shaping the House's approach to the regulation of Members' interests, or whether the introduction of the Register in 1974 indicated a departure on the part of parliamentarians from the tenets associated with the traditional belief in the House of Commons as a meeting place of gentlemen, with the historical claim to being 'the best club in London'.[10]

5 To be a Gentleman is not Enough: the Register

The Register of Members' Interests adopted by the House in 1974 was the product of a modern wave of concern over Members' interests which arose in the early 1960s. In this chapter we shall look at the Register and the events leading up to its adoption, and explore my argument that recent changes in the regulation of Members' interests are less fundamental than the apparent innovation of the Register would suggest.

The 1969 Select Committee: 'A Brief for the Status Quo'

As we discovered in chapter 4, Members' interests have rarely been included in the parliamentary agenda for debate. The 1969 Select Committee on Members' Interests (Declaration) was the most decisive move by the House on this subject since the Select Committee on Members of Parliament (Personal Interest) had carried out its limited review in 1896. Agitation by backbench Labour MPs in the early 1960s for further safeguards in the regulation of Members' interests had been ignored, and it is unlikely that the 1969 inquiry would have occurred had it not been for the Bagier affair, which raised delicate problems of propriety and personal judgment associated with trips organised and paid for by foreign interests, and linked them to the wider issue of declaration of interests.

In August 1968 the *Sunday Telegraph* had 'leaked' that Cabinet Ministers were considering legislation to force into the open political pressure group operators and professional lobbyists who tried to put pressure on MPs or civil servants, commenting that what had brought the issue to the forefront was the growing suspicion that vested interests were financing the welter of propaganda and counter-propaganda about the war in Nigeria; the Biafrans in particular were believed to be assisted by heavily-financed public relations firms. The press also gave a great deal of publicity to parliamentary visits to Rhodesia in this same winter, during which the position of the white minority was fully explained. However, it was the controversial Bagier affair which aroused most press interest at this time, and which the *Sunday Times* retrospectively singled out as the event which provoked the Wilson Government into setting up a Select Committee to investigate Members' interests.

The Bagier Affair

In mid-1967 the Greek colonels had employed a public relations firm – Maurice Fraser and Associates – to 'sell' Greece in Western Europe. Fraser had arranged for groups of people, including MPs, to visit Athens on trips paid for by the Greek Government. Fraser had to justify his costs to the Athens regime, and it was his 'fifth report' to Athens which led to legal action between Fraser and the *Sunday Times* before the latter were able to print the document on 6 October 1968.

The report became dynamite because in listing people concerned it referred to 'A British M.P., Lobbiest' (*sic*); and commented that, 'We have to disguise the identity of the British M.P. who is our lobbiest as this would compromise him. His name will be made available to the [Greek] Prime Minister'. Fraser maintained that the MP was unpaid and acted as 'linkman' between the Commons and Fraser's own office, alerting him whenever the topic of Greece cropped up in the House. Approached by the Press, Gordon Bagier (Lab) denied his involvement and dismissed the claim that Fraser had a British MP in the pay of the Greek Government as 'quite fantastic' (*Sunday Telegraph*, 6.10.1968). However, on 6 March 1969 the *This Week* programme on Thames Television also intimated that Bagier may have been the secret lobbyist in the Fraser Report. The next day *The Times* reported that Bagier had admitted visiting Greece at Fraser's invitation and that in May 1968 he had been invited by Fraser to accept a retainer as a Parliamentary Consultant, resigning in October 1968. Bagier insisted that he had not spoken in the House with reference to the situation in Greece, nor made any representations to any Government department.

He also widened the issue by going on to say, 'There are many MPs who combine their Membership with business or professional activities outside and this does not in any way affect their conduct as Members.'

(*The Times*, 7.3.1969). This is significant because, as we discovered in chapter 1, prospects for reform of the political process increase if the alleged act of wrongdoing can be linked to some basic defect in the system. In this case, the specific incident of the Bagier affair coincided with, and served to augment, the already growing lack of confidence in Parliament's existing methods for regulating Members' interests. Members who had previously been content to rely on the constraint of 'mutual trust' were stung into reconsidering the need for a register.

In his Diaries, Richard Crossman, Lord President of the House at the time of the Bagier scandal, confirms this conclusion. He also suggests that support for an inquiry into public relations activity was not unanimous in the Labour Cabinet. He recollects that Mr. Callaghan and Mr. Marsh had argued:

> What do we get out of this? All we shall do is expose the two or three other Labour MPs who may well have been working for PR firms. If we set up a Committee of Inquiry into this, don't we merely damage the Government at this stage?[1]

Despite government rhetoric that Members' interests are an issue for the House as a whole to decide, this clearly shows that the initiation of any action on which the House may have had to decide was considered tactically in terms of Government and Party advantage.

Debate on the Government motion setting up the Select Committee on Members' Interests (Declaration) and the accompanying motion nominating the Committee membership lasted for little more than two-and-a-quarter hours, reflecting the fact that it was now generally agreed that such a move was inevitable. The Committee membership was not so generally acceptable. Suspecting ulterior motives, several Labour backbenchers inquired why, with the exception of the Liberal Chief Whip, all the Members were Privy Councillors and all except one had, or had previously had, outside interests. The explanation that both Government and Opposition had thought it wise to nominate senior and experienced Members of the House on similar lines to the Committee of Privileges, did little to dissuade these Members from concluding it would be a 'safe committee' guaranteed to preserve the status quo. Although they were correct in observing that almost all the Committee members had some kind of interest, their criticism that 'the ordinary backbencher' was underrepresented does not necessarily follow. The implied assumption that the norm for a backbencher is not to have any kind of financial interest was not borne out by the Register which came into being in 1975. Nor did it necessary follow that a committee comprising mainly ex-Ministers would be 'softer' on declaration or registration of interests. Ministers, after all, are subject to an additional and much tougher code than backbenchers.

The Select Committee Report (*HC* 57: 1969)

The all-party Committee, chaired by the Rt. Hon. G.R. Strauss, held eleven meetings 'to consider the rules and practices of the House in relation to the declaration of Members' interests'. Without actually naming Bagier, they confirmed that it was an example of a Member acting as a consultant for a PR firm which had led to their appointment.

They received evidence on four 'related matters' which they judged lay outside their remit. The first was Members' remuneration. By excluding this they disregarded the possible connection between the low pay of Members and their tendency to pursue outside interests. Significantly this Committee sat before the first Report of the Top Salaries Review Body in 1971. The second exclusion was the fundamental question of whether MPs *ought* to have outside occupations in addition to their duties as MPs. Most witnesses had testified to the benefit derived by the House from the variety of knowledge and expertise gained from outside interests and the Committee had felt it unnecessary to pass judgment. Built into their Report, therefore, was the question-begging traditional assumption that it is proper for MPs to hold outside financial interests. The other two areas ruled out were the practices which govern, or should govern, the private interests of Ministers either while holding office or subsequently, and the specific workings of domestic or foreign organisations, firms, companies etc., except to the extent that the personal pecuniary interests of Members were involved.

In outlining the problem as they saw it, the Committee drew heavily on a Prime Ministerial statement of March 1969, which had identified two separate strands to the problem: one was the position of MPs who by virtue of a prior connection with a domestic or overseas body, were involved in matters which were the concern of Parliament and Government; the second related to the operation of public relations and other organisations holding an account or commission on behalf of an overseas Government or an overseas political interest (*HC Debs* 780:1969, 1630–9).

The remainder of their report was presented in three parts: a survey of the relevant law, practice and procedure of Parliament and consideration of its adequacy today; consideration of new machinery which might improve present practices (i.e. a register); and consideration of a code of conduct for Members.

The Committee's comments on the adequacy of existing rules and conventions provide a valuable insight into their perception of the problem. They found the resolutions of the House restricting professional advocacy too narrow to provide a clear code of conduct for Members who belonged to professions other than the Bar, and still less for Members with more tenuous connections with outside interests. Highlighting the problem of public relations activity they warned of the temptation to extend the role of retained Member from one of advice (which was acceptable) to one of advocacy (which was not). They found the practice and procedure of the House on voting with a pecuniary interest obscure but believed that to replace Mr. Speaker Abbot's ruling of 1811 with a standing order defining 'pecuniary interest' would be impractical and too rigid, and might even facilitate the improper use of votes.

Their chief criticism concerned the imprecise custom of declaration of interest. Current practice raised two particular problems: firstly, what kind of interest should be declared; and secondly, when should an interest be declared? The custom of declaration had not been dealt with by Erskine May or the manual of procedure, largely because of the prevalent assumption that Hon. Members can be relied upon to assess such delicate matters in an honourable way and that detailed rules are undesirable and unnecessary. Although sharing this assumption, the Committee felt that if rules had to exist they should provide a clear and comprehensive guide.

They considered registration of interests as a possible solution and the evidence received fell predominantly into two groups: proposals for Members to register their interests; and proposals for outside persons or organisations to register details of payments or benefits made available to Members. They decided, however, that a voluntary register would be an impractical basis for registering the interests of Members generally, in contrast to one confined to Members of a small party (such as the Liberal Party Register[2]), while a compulsory register, with its implication of sanctions, would carry the possibility of placing the House in the difficult position of having to discipline its own Members.

On balance they concluded:

> All the registers so far considered would expose to the public view much more information than is declared under the House's present custom of declaring an interest. The object of that custom is, or should be, to inform Members and the public of any financial interest touching an issue which is currently the subject of a Member's speech or action. It does not require declaration of financial interests irrelevant to their purpose . . . a general register is directed to the contingency that an interest *might* affect a Member's action. The House's practice is, or should be, aimed at revealing an interest when it does affect it. (para 74)

Accordingly they dismissed the possibility of a register not on legalistic or technical grounds – though they said they could have listed even more of such grounds than those given in evidence – but primarily on objections of principle.

With regard to proposals for outside organisations to register details of payments or benefits made available to Members, they noted that the Institute of Public Relations intended to seek legislation which would require *all* public relations consultants to obtain a licence to practice and hoped that, when Parliament was invited to consider such legislation, a statutory code of conduct would be included which would specifically require the public disclosure of any employment on parliamentary matters, with the MP indicating the object of the employment and the remuneration to be paid (para 86).

Having rejected registration in favour of strengthening the traditional procedures of the House, the Committee recommended what they considered to be a comprehensive code of conduct to guide Members in the discharge of their duties. Kept under periodic review by the Committee of Privileges and backed up by the sanction that a serious violation could be construed as a contempt of the House (para 117) the Committee believed this to be the most effective solution to the dilemma of conflict of interest confronting MPs.

To give effect to the code of conduct they recommended the House adopt two resolutions. Firstly:

> That in any debate or proceeding of the House or its committees or transactions or communications which a Member may have with other Members, or with Ministers or servants of the Crown, he shall disclose any relevant pecuniary interest or benefit of whatever nature, whether direct or indirect, that he may have had, may have or may be expecting to have. (para 103)

This would have the effect of formalising and extending practices which had a historical base, by turning the convention of declaration into a resolution of the House. The words 'or benefit of whatever nature' included in the resolution were indicative of the Committee's desire to broaden the interpretation of 'interest' to cover the growing spectrum of modern rewards, and were expressly intended to cover journeys abroad and associated benefits.

Secondly, they recommended that the House should extend its prohibition on advocacy to all forms of professional and analogous activities by adopting the resolution:

> That it is contrary to the usage and derogatory to the dignity of the House that a Member should bring forward by speech or question, or advocate in this House or among his fellow Members any bill, motion, matter or cause for a fee, payment, retainer or reward, direct or indirect, which he has received, is receiving or expects to receive. (para 110)

The viability of this resolution turned upon the possibility of distinguishing between advocacy of a specific measure in Parliament for a fee or retainer, and the advancement of an argument by a Member who, through a continuing association with an industry, service or concern from which he might obtain some remuneration (for example, trade union sponsorship), is able to draw upon specialist knowledge of the subject under debate. This was a fine distinction traditionally upheld by the House, but one which the committee thought *could* be construed by the Committee of Privileges if it became necessary.

With hindsight the Committee's assessment of the situation seems unduly complacent, but the Clerk to the Committee recalled that at the time the ultimate answer – a register – did not ever look like commending itself, even after the Committee had closely examined the American experience.

Parliamentary response: a reassertion of tradition

Outside of Parliament the Report received a rough ride from the press, who were generally critical of the Committee's adherence to the assumption that on the matter of privacy MPs should be treated no differently from private citizens. This belief, the *Sunday Times* (21.12.1969) argued, rendered the Committee blind to the fundamental justification for disclosure, 'that MPs are public men elected by the public to serve the public interest'.

Inside Parliament the Report created little excitement and in fact was never debated in the House.[3] The spirit of moral fervour which had surrounded the inception of the Committee had subsided. The Labour Government did not reach a conclusion on its proposals before the June 1970 General Election and the incoming Conservative Government was even less inclined to give the Select Committee Report any priority; nor were they pressed to do so by backbenchers. Significantly the new Parliament contained at least 218 Members with readily identifiable business interests, the overwhelming majority of these being Conservative MPs. It took four months for the Conservative Government to reach a decision on the Report. Already its unwilling custodian, they were able to exploit the shaky distinction underlying the Committee's resolution on advocacy by Members in order to inform the House that incurable defects in the resolution prevented the Government from recommending them (*HC Debs* 805:1970, 214–5).

The significance of parliamentary and Government inactivity on the issue of Members' interests following the Report should not be overlooked. In chapter 1 I argued that the failure of an élite to act or make decisions is in itself often of greater importance than the decisions they do make, and non-decision-making can in itself be a manifestation of bias. In this instance, not only was bias created by individuals, such as the Leader of the House, making choices between the alternatives of introducing formalised rules and relying on the 'good sense' of

Members; it was also sustained by the prevailing traditional ethos and practices of the House, which informed individual decisions and continued to encourage trust in the honour and self-restraint of individual Members, along with a belief in their right to privacy.

The issue of Members' interests remained dormant until the Top Salaries Review Body reported in December 1971 and accepted the argument that Members should be regarded as working on a full-time basis. Several Labour MPs, disturbed by the facts disclosed in the Boyle Report about the extent of Members' outside activities attempted to exploit the Government's acceptance of these proposals as an opportunity to reopen discussions on disclosure of MPs' outside interests and remuneration. The willingness of the Leader of the House to allow this suggests a shift in the Government's attitude following the Boyle Report, but this was not rapidly translated into overt action.

In fact nothing more occurred on the subject until rumours concerning the involvement of MPs in the Poulson affair began to surface in July 1972. The extent to which the Poulson affair changed opinion in the House was best summed up for me by a House of Commons Clerk who explained:

> Before that [the Poulson affair] I believed that the vast majority of Members thought that some kind of patchwork on the lines of the 1969 Committee's recommendations was quite enough; what was needed was to apply and underline traditional House practices. During and after the affair, it was a different story; a Register of Interests became inevitable.

The resolutions on declaration and registration of Members' interests which eventually emerged in 1974 were primarily the outcome of another 'issue-attention cycle' in the history of Members' interests; this time triggered off by the Poulson affair.

The Poulson Affair: The Parliamentary Repercussions[4]

Mr. John Poulson was an architect who developed his practice to set up a chain of business companies: property management consultancies, a construction company, 'Open Systems Building', and an export promotion business. From a single architectural practice in Pontefract he came to own the largest architectural practice in Europe, with a turnover of £1 million a year and a staff of 750 people. His bankruptcy petition was filed on 4 January 1972. On 13 June his public examination in bankruptcy began and it then emerged that this remarkable business achievement owed much to an elaborate network of politicians and public sector employees. He was expelled for professional misconduct from the Royal Institute of British Architects in November 1972.

The first hint of Poulson's activities appeared in the *Bradford Telegraph and Argus*.[5] It caused little comment at the time, but sparked off a series of foraging articles by *Private Eye*. When the public bankruptcy hearing began, and the risk of libel diminished, the rest of the media took up the story. The Poulson revelations raised the question of payments to people in public life and created anxiety about the apparent involvement of the civil service and local government. They also rekindled concern about the vexed question of Members' business interests.

On 9 July 1972 the *Observer* carried the headline 'PR men say 20 to 30 MPs are "bendable"'. The same edition carried a feature article on MPs' public roles and private interests which emphasised the role that 'scandals' played in stimulating Parliament to take action on the issue of Members' interests:

> NOT AGAIN! Every few years, scandalous allegations of corruption and financial malpractices by MPs are made. There is a great fuss, and an inquiry is set on foot to allay public disquiet. Its report may or may not exculpate the MP concerned, but it nearly always raises interesting issues about the relationship of MPs and outside interests, whether they are commercial firms, foreign Governments or public relations consultants. There is desultory discussion about what should be done to regularise matters, then the issue is dropped until the next scandal breaks.

Inside the House, MPs' complacency was undoubtedly jolted by the Poulson affair. The Prime Minister was sufficiently alarmed by the magnitude of the Poulson network to assure the House in July 1972 that the Director of Public Prosecutions had instructed the Metropolitan Police to conduct an investigation into the affair in order to discover if there were any grounds for criminal proceedings (*HC Debs* 841:1972, 402–8). Until this investigation was complete, he refused to set up any other type of inquiry, select committee or royal commission. He also announced the resignation of the Home Secretary, Mr. Maudling,[6] whose name, along with three other MPs,[7] had been mentioned during the bankruptcy hearings. Although Mr. Maudling had stressed that his connections with Poulson were above reproach, he nevertheless felt it inappropriate to continue as Home Secretary (and therefore ultimate police authority for the metropolis) while the Metropolitan Police conducted their inquiry.

In June 1973, as a result of this inquiry the Attorney General signed fiats authorising proceedings under the Prevention of Corruption Acts against Mr. John Poulson and a civil servant, Mr. George Pottinger.[8] On 11 February 1974 Mr. Poulson and Mr. Pottinger were convicted on various offences under the Prevention of Corruption Acts and, with subsequent prosecutions, a vast network of corruption was gradually revealed, involving local government at both district and county level, nationalised industries, the National Health Service, the civil service, central government departments and, although none was prosecuted, Members of Parliament.[9]

Whereas the House had been able to bury the issue of Members' interests after the 1969 Select Committee had reported, the series of prosecutions for corruption resulting from the Poulson affair and further events, such as the Lonrho scandal,[10] kept the wider issue of standards of conduct in public life very much alive throughout 1973 and 1974. In this climate the House could not easily avoid reflection on the adequacy of its own safeguards against conflict of interest and corruption. Viewing the problem primarily as a House matter, the Conservative Government had initiated inter-party talks in February 1973 to discover how best to deal with what they now viewed as a very difficult and complicated problem (*HC Debs* 849:1973, 1622). These inter-party talks continued throughout the rest of the session, extended into the 1973–74 session and were still in progress when Parliament was dissolved in February 1974.

During these talks both parties had independently formed proposals for future action. A sub-committee of the Parliamentary Labour Party[11] recommended both a compulsory register of Members' interests to be kept in security by the Speaker, and a code of disclosure. At a sparsely attended meeting of the PLP on 9 May 1973 these proposals were accepted, with the modification (passed by 28 votes to 9) that the register be *public. The Times* (29.6.1973) reported that the Leader of the House, Mr. Prior, had surprised the Conservative 1922 Committee with plans for a voluntary register, in conjunction with proposals for a code of conduct, and that only three of the 17 backbenchers who commented on his announcement gave unreserved support. Proposals for a voluntary register remained however, an empty gesture, and were lost with the defeat of the Conservative Party at the General Election in February 1974.

A Change of Government – And a Change of Direction?

Although Mr. Wilson announced to the Commons his intention to appoint a Royal Commission to inquire into Standards of Conduct in Public Life,[12] the new Labour Cabinet were reported to be more lukewarm towards proposals for a compulsory register than they had been when in Opposition (*Guardian*, 19.4.1974). Several events coincided which hastened their decision to put proposals for both declaration and compulsory registration of interests before the House in May 1974.

In April 1974 a complaint of breach of privilege was raised concerning the allegation, broadcast on radio, by Mr. Joe Ashton (Lab) that a number of MPs had surrendered their freedom of action as parliamentarians to outside bodies (*HC Debs* 872:1974, 783–6). Referred to the Committee of Privileges, this matter had embarrassing repercussions for the Government because the Leader of the House, Mr. Short, who would normally have chaired the Committee, had issued a public statement that in January 1963 he had accepted payment from Mr. T. Dan Smith, who was later jailed for corruption during the Poulson trials.[13]

Mr. Ashton's remarks coincided with the publication of the Report from the Prime Minister's Committee on Local Government Rules of Conduct (Cmnd 5636:1974). While concerned with local government, this Report publicly set out many of the arguments for and against a register of interests which were also being raised with regard to Parliament and came out in favour of establishing a compulsory register.

In addition to these by-products of the Poulson affair, both the *Guardian* on 11 May 1974 and the *Sunday Telegraph* on 12 May reported Mr. Brian Walden's (Lab) disclosure that he was retained by the National Association of Bookmakers, at a fee of £5,000 a year for five years, to act as a political consultant. While he had not concealed his work for the bookmakers, it may have surprised MPs and constituents alike to learn that the amount of the payment was more than he was paid in his representative capacity.

Against this background of increasing unease about Members' interests, and with the likelihood of another General Election in the near future, it became electorally important for Labour to take the initiative to reassure the public about standards of conduct in Parliament. They did so by presenting the House with proposals, based on those approved by the PLP in 1973, for both a public compulsory register of interests, and for a rule requiring disclosure of relevant pecuniary interests or benefits in any debate or proceeding of the House or its Committees, and in any transactions or communications a Member might have with other Members, Ministers or servants of the Crown.

The 1974 Debate: '. . . A Sort of Gentleman Versus Players Match'

The Labour Government's proposals for registration and declaration of Members' interests were accepted by the House on 22 May 1974 (*HC Debs* 874:1974, 391–544). In effect, at the end of a seven-hour debate, the House had resolved to turn the traditional *convention* of declaration of interest into a more comprehensive *rule* of the House, and had agreed to the principle of public, general disclosure of interests in the form of a compulsory register of Members' outside financial interests.

We should not miss the particular irony of events whereby the Register was commended to the House by Mr. Short, Leader of the House, who as we have seen, had himself had to admit to having received a gift from one of Mr. Poulson's associates.

Although the official party whips were off duty during this debate, party discipline rests at least partly on group opinion and group loyalty. The number of Members going through the lobbies was high for a free vote and though complicated by tactical motives, their voting behaviour contradicted Government rhetoric claiming Members' interests to be a House rather than a party issue. There were in practice distinct party clusterings.

An amendment reflecting the feeling of the 1922 Committee, to the effect that interests should be declared if the individual Member judged his interest as one which would be regarded by the House as relevant to the matter under discussion, was defeated by 336 votes to 221 (Table 6, Appendix 4). Approximately 75 per cent of Conservative MPs supported the amendment, which would have preserved the role of discretion of the individual MP, and 96 per cent of Labour MPs voted against. New Conservative Members who had entered the House at the February 1974 General Election showed a greater tendency to vote against the amendment than those Conservative MPs with longer parliamentary service (Table 7, Appendix 4). The Government's motion on declaration of interests was agreed without division.

The motion establishing a compulsory public register was carried by 365 votes to 170, giving a larger Government majority than expected (Table 8, Appendix 4). Again there was distinct party clustering, with 94 per cent of the Labour Party supporting a compulsory register compared to 21 per cent of the Conservative Party. The 57 per cent of Conservative MPs who voted against the motion included Mr. Edward Heath and at least seven members of the Shadow Cabinet, among them, Mrs. Margaret Thatcher. In this division, Conservative MPs who entered the House in February 1974 showed a greater tendency to vote for a compulsory register than their colleagues with longer service (Table 9, Appendix 4), but this trend needs to be viewed in context. Among the 62 Conservatives who joined the 208 Labour Members in supporting the Register were also several Opposition front-bench spokesmen. By May 1974 a greater number of Conservative Members had gradually, if unwillingly, conceded that it would be a reassuring gesture to take some action to restore the good name of the House.

The Government's third motion, setting up a select committee to consider the arrangements for implementing the resolutions concerning declaration and registration of interests was agreed without division. With a majority in favour of establishing a compulsory register, Mr. Prior's amendment, proposing that the substantive decision between compulsory and voluntary registration should be left to the consideration of the Select Committee, automatically fell.

About 50 Members took part in this debate on Members' interests and among the numerous opinions and anxieties expressed, two particular subjects dominated. Firstly, despite the Leader of the House's warning that the issue was *not* whether MPs should have outside interests, but whether and how they should be disclosed, much of the discussion focused on whether MPs should be full-time or part-time Members. Both the substance of this issue and its relevancy or otherwise to the problem of conflict of interest were contested. With few exceptions traditionalist Conservative MPs defended the possession of outside interests, on the grounds that a Parliament consisting of whole-time professional politicians would lose both its character and independence and would become out of touch with the lives of those for whom it legislates. Labour MPs, on the other hand, while not unanimous among themselves, argued for a professional full-time House of Commons; drawing support from the Boyle Committee's recommendation that MPs should be paid on the basis of full-time membership. MPs have not yet resolved whether being a Member of Parliament in Britain is an amateur or professional occupation[14] and Mr. Max Madden (Lab) illustrated the tension in the House between the two different philosophies informing the status ascribed to membership when he observed, 'an attempt has been made to present this debate as a sort of gentleman versus players match' (*HC Debs* 874:1974, 501).

The second dominant issue was the effect of the register on Members' privacy. Opinion continued to be divided as to whether a Member was entitled to the same degree of privacy as an ordinary citizen, or whether on taking up public office he should expect to sacrifice a certain amount of personal privacy. An effective speech on this issue was made by Brian Walden (Lab) who viewed the Register as a 'gross and palpable intrusion' into a Member's privacy, but advocated disclosure on the grounds that:

> If my experience of life is any guide, there is nothing so disappointing to the prurient as a revelation. Once they actually know what is going on, their interest in it will subside rapidly. The suspicious will go to lusher pastures where someone is trying to conceal something . . . once we have a public register the whole thing will die in a year or two. (*HC Debs* 874:1974, 456)

My random sample interviews with MPs suggest that Mr. Walden's persuasive speech prompted some of the tactical voting which took place during the division on the compulsory register, whereby some MPs voted for the register not because they wanted it, but because they thought this would be the quickest way to kill off the whole idea.

The 1974 Committee Report (*HC* 102: 1974)

Whereas the 1969 Committee had been concerned with the *principles* of declaration and registration and had therefore been composed more like a Privilege Committee, this Committee was more of a working committee, concerned with putting into operation decisions already approved by the House. Only three members were Privy Councillors. It was reappointed with largely the same membership after the General Election in October 1974, when the Labour Government was returned with a narrow majority of three seats over all other Members.

The Committee identified two different types of issue on which they were required to make recommendations: the administrative and procedural problems involved in both resolutions, which were largely technical and unlikely to prove controversial; and the quite separate political problems associated with registration. Their most difficult task was determining the scope of the Register. Taking remuneration to include taxable expenses, allowances or benefits as well as direct income, they recommended the registration of nine specific classes of pecuniary interest or benefit which they emphasised were broad guidelines within which Members should 'proceed with good sense and responsibility'. These categories, which later formed the basis of the registration requirement, were as follows:

(1) remunerated directorships of companies, public or private;
(2) remunerated employments or offices;
(3) remunerated trades, professions or vocations;
(4) the names of clients when the interests referred to above include personal services by the Member which arise out of or are related in any manner to his membership of the House;
(5) financial sponsorships, (a) as a Parliamentary candidate where to the knowledge of the Member the sponsorship in any case exceeds 25 per cent of the candidate's election expenses, or (b) as a Member of Parliament, by any person or organisation, stating whether any such sponsorship includes any payment to the Member or any material benefit or advantage direct or indirect;
(6) overseas visits relating to or arising out of membership of the House where the cost of any such visit has not been wholly borne by the Member or by public funds;
(7) any payments or any material benefits or advantages received from or on behalf of foreign Governments, organisations or persons;
(8) land and property of substantial value or from which a substantial income is derived;
(9) the names of companies or other bodies in which the Member has, to his knowledge, either himself or with or on behalf of his spouse or infant children, a beneficial interest in shareholdings of a nominal value greater than one-hundredth of the issue share capital. (para 13)

Sensitive to Members' privacy they did not recommend the disclosure of the amounts of any remuneration or benefits received, nor the interests of spouses or children except in certain arrangements concerning shareholdings. This was intended as a register of the sources or nature of pecuniary interests and benefits which might be thought to affect the conduct of an MP in his parliamentary capacity, *not* a public income tax return designed to indicate the magnitude of a Member's income.

The essence of their proposals was a permanent select committee on Members' interests which, in conjunction with its Clerk, the Registrar of Members' interests, would monitor how the Register worked in practice, deal with *ad hoc* problems and complaints, and keep under review the whole subject of Members' interests. Unlike the House and Senate Ethics Committees in America under the Ethics in Government Act 1978,[15] the Registrar and his staff were not envisaged as enforcement officers. The Committee made it clear that the philosophy of the House remained one of trust, each Member being individually responsible for completing the registration form and ensuring its accuracy. The ultimate sanction behind the obligation to register was that it had been imposed by resolution of the House and therefore either a refusal to comply with registration or the wilful provision of misleading or inaccurate information might be considered a contempt of the House.

They advised that compulsory registration should be restricted to MPs, but recommended the question of registering interests of all parliamentary candidates be referred to the next Speaker's Conference on Electoral Law, with a view to introducing legislation before the next general election.[16]

The Select Committee Report was not debated in the House until 12 June 1975, six months after it was published. After a three-hour debate, the Government's main motion agreeing with the Committee's recommendations on registration and proposing to establish such a register as soon as possible was carried on a free vote by 183 votes to 23 (Table 10, Appendix 4). Again distinct party clusterings were evident. Three-quarters of those supporting the motion were Labour MPs, and with three exceptions, all of those voting against were Conservatives. Compared to 1974 when over 80 per cent of Members eligible to vote had taken part in both divisions, the participation rate in this division was poor, with only one-third of MPs eligible to vote actually doing so.

Comparison is made difficult by the covert management of the timetable through the usual channels, but the lack of interest exhibited in June 1975 as compared to the previous year is consistent with the pattern of an 'issue-attention cycle'. The well-attended 1974 debate occurred at the peak of an attention cycle concerning Members' financial interests and the Select Committee expected there to be considerable public interest in their report. However, by the time it was debated, anxiety concerning Members' interests had largely subsided. Also Members were no longer having to consider their image in the context of a pending general election as they had been in 1974. As my interviews with MPs confirmed, in June 1975 MPs were less pressured to take an interest in, or be seen to take an interest in, the reform of internal procedures relating to Members' financial interests. Poor attendance also reflected the fact that this debate was simply concerned with implementing principles already agreed by the House.

The Register in Operation

The first edition of the Register, printed in accordance with replies received by the Registrar of Members' Interests, was published in November 1975 (*HC* 699). Approximately 87 per cent of Members made an entry under one or more of the nine specific categories of registrable interests. The balance of Members registered 'nil', with the exception of Mr. Enoch Powell. The entry against his name stated simply that he had not returned the form for the registration of interests. Of the 84 MPs who registered 'nil' interests, 63 were Labour, ten Conservative, two Liberal and nine belonged to minor parties. The percentage of each of the two main parties recording at least one entry under each heading is shown in Table 3.

With the one exception of category 5 (financial sponsorship), where the higher percentage of Labour than Conservative Members reflected Labour's traditional link with the trade unions, a larger percentage of Conservative than Labour Members recorded at least one entry under each of the nine specific categories of registrable interests. The long association of the Conservative Party with business was well in evidence with approximately 55 per cent of Conservative as opposed to 8 per cent of Labour MPs making an entry under category 1 (directorships), Conservative MP Mr. Arthur Jones topping the league with 36 directorships. Party differences were less evident under category 6, with approximately 20 per cent of the Labour Party and 23 per cent of the Conservative Party recording one or more overseas visits. Few Members of either party had interests to disclose under category 4 (clients), or category 7 (payments from abroad). Correspondingly, these two categories were the lowest in the league table of categories as measured by the percentage of the House as a whole who recorded at least one entry. Top of the league was category 3 (trades or professions etc.), with approximately 42 per cent of the whole House recording an entry here.

Table 3

Classified entries in the Register as on 1 November 1975

Abbreviated heading in Register	Lab MPs		Con MPs		Whole House	
	no.	%	no.	%	no.	%
1. Directorships	25	7.9	151	54.5	187	29.4
2. Employment or Office	38	11.9	91	32.9	136	21.4
3. Trades or Professions etc	96	30.2	155	56.0	268	42.2
4. Clients	7	2.2	16	5.8	23	3.6
5. Financial Sponsorship	157	49.4	2	0.7	160	25.2
6. Overseas visits	65	20.4	64	23.1	132	20.8
7. Payments from abroad	12	3.8	14	5.1	27	4.6
8. Land and Property	14	4.4	61	22.0	81	12.8
9. Declarable Shareholdings	17	5.3	88	31.8	108	17.0

Source: Compiled by the author from the Register Members' Interests as on 1 November 1975, *HC* 699.

Notes The total number of MPs for each heading is the number of MPs who have made one or more entries under that heading. It does not record the amount of entries each MP made under that heading. As Members could have entries under more than one heading, the percentage columns will not total 100 per cent. As the percentages are of the whole party, not simply the backbench party, they do not take account of the fact that Ministers – in 1975, Labour – cannot hold directorships. The percentage of a party holding directorships when that party forms the Government is likely to be lower than when that party is out of office.

While illustrating the spread of Members' self-admitted outside financial interests as shown by the Register, these statistics provide only some of the detail. Bearing in mind that the Register has been accused of being more revealing for its omissions than for its actual content, it is likely that even this formidable list of categories is far from exhaustive of the personal or sectional interests which may give rise to conflict of interest problems. A survey of the *content* of the entries reveals vast differences in the nature or extent of interests that are classified under a particular heading. It also reveals the inconsistencies in style and content of the entries. Registration is the responsibility of each individual Member and as we saw in chapter 1, Members' perception or judgment as to what constitutes a registrable interest will inevitably vary.

The press speculated that several Members had been able to circumvent the spirit of the Register and quite legitimately either give a deceptive picture of their interests or register no interests at all. Some discussion of the examples seized upon by the press, along with others taken directly from the Register or from conversations with MPs helps to illustrate the most obvious gaps and anomalies.

Directorships This category was widely interpreted by Members and encompassed entries referring to paid directorships, unpaid directorships, non-executive directorships and chairmanships; the exact nature of these was not always made clear. More importantly there was the problem of directorships of holding companies. Some MPs felt obliged to provide a full list of subsidary companies, while others judged it sufficient simply to record the name of the company. A further limitation of this category was illustrated by Mr. Tom Normanton's (Con) comment to Andrew Roth[17] that although he held 14 chairmanships and directorships only four were listed in the Register. All the others were non-remunerative posts and therefore none of them *had* to be included in the Register.

Employment or Office In some instances Members appeared to find that this category overlapped with Directorships. For example, having listed 'Slater Walker (Middle East) (Managing Director)' and 'Slater Walker (Lebanon) (Managing Director)' under Directorships, Mr. Jonathan Aitken (Con) then recorded 'as above' under the next heading of Employment or Office. Also Members who were parliamentary advisers or consultants appeared to be divided as to whether these interests should be recorded under Employment or Office or under Financial Sponsorship.

Clients Here there appeared to be confusion over whether MPs should list the clients of companies with which they were associated. For example, while Mr. Patrick McNair-Wilson (Con) listed the 15 clients of his public relations company, Mr. Michael Roberts (Con) adjudged that a statement of his connection with a public relations firm, John Addey Associates, was sufficient disclosure. Solicitor Bruce Douglas-Mann (Lab) illustrated the practical problem of trying to distinguish clearly between those clients with whom a Member has a relationship *qua* Member and which have to be registered, and those who deal with a Member in his private capacity and do not have to be registered. After the listing the clients of his law firm he added: 'No remuneration received from clients for anything done in my capacity as Member. But the clients occasionally supply information that is useful in my parliamentary work or express views which, when I agree with them, I may reiterate.'

Financial Sponsorship This category mainly attracted entries concerning trade-union sponsorship and MPs seemed unclear about how much they should reveal. Illustrating this point, the *Sunday Times* (30.11. 1975) observed that Eric Moonman (Lab) listed financial sponsorship by the National Graphical Association both as a candidate and as a Member, without putting a figure on the sponsorship, while in contrast, Mr. John Cronin (Lab) said that the Confederation of Health Services Employees contributed £500 per annum to his constituency Labour Party.

Material Benefits While obliged to record their remuneration from employment or directorships, Members were not required to disclose other 'material benefits or advantages' unless these came from abroad. So, as the *Sunday Times* (30.11.1975) pointed out, if an MP was the recipient, Mr. John Poulson's practice of providing free architectural services and in some cases building houses, would not have to be recorded under any of the nine specific categories in the Register.

Land and Property Anomalies concerning land and property derived largely from the fact that the appropriate rule did not define what constituted land of 'substantial value' requiring disclosure. The Committee had preferred to leave the interpretation of phrases such as 'material benefits or advantages', 'substantial value' and 'substantial income' to the judgment and discretion of the individual Member, rather than laying down fixed rules or amounts. While some Members felt obliged to record their homes as property interests, other Members with more valuable properties and with a different assessment of what amounted to substantial value were able legitimately to record a 'nil' interest. Even where Members provided information regarding their substantial property holdings this was frequently unhelpful. For example, although Mr. William Whitelaw (Con) was within the requirements of the Register when he recorded that 'I still retain a comparatively small amount of land near Glasgow, the ownership being mainly in the hands of my daughters', the usefulness of his entry appears dubious when compared with the following extract of his interests contained in Andrew Roth's 1975–76 edition of *The Business Background of MPs*:

Landowner:	Woodhall estate near Kirkintilloch, near Glasgow (with wife made three applications for outline planning permission in 1973).
Farmer:	300 Acres, Ennim, near Penrith, Cumberland (raises beef).
Co-owner:	Mount Pleasant at Blencowe, near Penrith (with one of Europe's leading herds of Charolais cattle).

Declarable Shareholdings The Register required Members to declare their shareholdings *only* when this amounted to more than 1 per cent of the company's nominal value. Thus, Mr. Alan Clarke (Con) whose shareholdings were listed in Andrew Roth's book as 'nothing over the value of £10,000 in any one company, apart from six $10,000 shares in Woods Petroleum field in Brunei' did not need to record any of his shareholdings in the Register. While few MPs were willing to support a more stringent formula for shareholdings, most were aware of the anomalies the 1 per cent rule gave rise to.

Non-pecuniary interests The Register was, and still is, exclusively concerned with financial interests. The majority (over 80 per cent) of MPs I talked to in my random sample considered it would be impractical to register and/or declare non-financial interests, although most of them thought that such interests could alter a Member's judgment. As one Conservative Member commented, 'where do you draw the line. You shop at the Co-op, is this an interest?' To require disclosure of non-pecuniary interests – for example, where Members educate their children – would not only create difficulties of definition and regulation, but, as several Members in the sample pointed out, would also alter the balance between privacy and publicity; a contentious issue which has been seen to be central to the debate over disclosure.

Since the publication of the first edition of the Register, the Select Committee on Members' Interests has periodically issued additional guidelines on registration. Among the more interesting changes or points of clarification are the following:

> *Directorships* Where a Member's directorship of a company requires him to be a director of other subsidiary companies, he is advised to disclose in the Register the names of the subsidiary companies. (*HC* 479: 1976)
>
> *Functions* Following a complaint by a Member that a loophole in the disclosure procedures allowed the catering facilities of the House to be abused, any Member who sponsors a function in the Palace of Westminster from which sponsorship he derives a taxable benefit is required to declare the source of the benefit. (*HC* 337: 1980)

Gifts In response to the criticism that the specific category of gifts from domestic sources had been overlooked, the Committee had stated in 1975 (*HC* 677) that the general reference to 'any pecuniary interest or other material benefit' in the introduction to the Register clearly included gifts. However, five years later they found it necessary to clarify the registration of gifts still further and advised that the receipt of a gift in relation to an MP's parliamentary duties, other than from overseas to which category 7 applied, should be registered under subsection (b) of category 5, Financial Sponsorship (*HC* 337: 1980).

Relatives

It was largely sensitivity to Members' privacy which led the 1974 Select Committee to exclude the interests of a Member's spouse and children from registration, and ten years later the current Select Committee on Members' Interests had firmly upheld this principle. The context was the 'Omani affair' which aroused accusations of a conflict of interest between the Prime Minister's official role and her son Mark's commercial interests. Having investigated whether the Prime Minister's conduct on her 'batting for Britain' tour of Oman in 1981 affected the Register of Interests, the Select Committee rejected the complaint of a Labour backbencher, Mr. Brian Sedgemore, that the Prime Minister had failed to declare an interest over the £300 million Oman University contract won by Cementation International, a British construction company by whom her son was allegedly employed as a consultant. It also rejected a second complaint that she failed to declare an interest when answering parliamentary questions. Mrs. Thatcher had refused to provide information on the nature and extent of Mark's involvement in the contract on grounds of 'family privacy'. The Select Committee confirmed: 'While Members are required to register their own pecuniary interests, there is no requirement, except in one case regarding shareholdings to register the interests of spouses, infant children or other close relatives.' (*HC* 330: 26.3.1984)

This case raises the general issue of the interests of Members' spouses and children. Indirectly it also prompted this writer to speculate whether the financial interests and activities of spouses are more likely to be problematic for women MPs than for their male colleagues, an increasingly relevant question given the growth in two-career families with the wife actively involved in politics. Coincidentally, controversy and innuendo surrounding the tax affairs and business activities of the husband of Geraldine Ferraro, the Democratic vice-presidential candidate in America, lends weight to this reflection. The 'Omani affair' also illustrates the fact that a situation involving apparent conflict of interest provides scope for accusations of improper motives. No suggestion of corruption need actually be present for rumour and innuendo to fester. Rather than simply echoing the opinions of its predecessor committee, the current Select Committee on Members' Interests could more usefully consider whether some firm guidelines concerning the financial interests of spouses, children and close relatives would serve to avoid further debatable incidents or associations of this type. Mrs. Thatcher's involvement in this affair was all the more embarrassing because it called into question not only the conduct of MPs, but also the more stringent rules regulating the behaviour of Ministers. And as Mr. Peter Shore (Lab) was quick to point out, the latter rules lie within the control of the Prime Minister herself.

The Register: Innovation or Extension of Tradition?

> In taking this step the House broke sharply with its own past and recognised that in modern conditions the old 'honour system' which left the declaration of an interest entirely to the discretion of the individual Member no longer afforded the House sufficient protection from suspicion. *Financial Times* (9.1.1975)

How far did the acceptance of the 1974/1975 resolutions concerning declaration and registration of Members' interests indicate a genuine change in the House's approach to conflict of interest from the traditional attitude identified in chapter 4?

As far as the principle of the matter was concerned, several changes occurred. Firstly, the resolution in May 1974 concerning declaration of interest implemented a procedural change by converting what had previously been a convention into a rule of the House, and one which covered past and future as well as present interests. In doing so, it in theory removed the prerogative of the *individual* Member to be the sole judge of the relevancy of interests to be declared, and entrusted this to the *collective* wisdom of the House.

Secondly, the acceptance of a register of interests suggests a change in the attitude of the House towards disclosure. As we saw in chapter 4, the House has traditionally been protective of the individual Member's privacy, and has required disclosure of interests only at the point of speaking or voting on a matter upon which his action may be influenced by his personal interest. While the Register was conceived of as supplementary to, and not in place of this form of disclosure, which continued to be embodied in the rule of declaration of interests, it introduced a different approach to disclosure. This approach, which had previously been rejected by the 1969 Select Committee on Members' Interests, holds that disclosure should be general, comprehensive and public and concedes the right of the public, in addition to other Members, to general surveillance of a Member's private interests. It involves trading off some of a Member's right to privacy in favour of greater publicity. However, it is doubtful whether the primary reason for establishing the Register was the democratically inspired one of providing the public with information on Members' interests. Statements by successive Leaders of the House putting the case for registration suggest that it was conceived more in terms of protecting Members' from gossip and innuendo and in restoring the good name of the House, than as a means of avoiding actual conflicts of interest or as a punitive measure imposed on Members collectively.

Mr. Enoch Powell argues that the resolution concerning registration did indeed introduce a change, in that the House was purporting to change the law of the land and restrict eligibility to the House by mere resolution of the House. This, he argues, is unconstitutional because 'it confuses the effect of a resolution of the House, which is internal to the House, with legislation, which changes the law of the land and in which the House only participates' (*HC Debs* 893:1975, 745). The validity of this idiosyncratic view, which is explored further in chapter 6, remains a matter of opinion, and it is unclear how many MPs, if any, share his view.

Despite these apparent shifts in principle or procedure, very little has changed in *practice* in the House's appraisal of and approach towards the regulation of Members' interests. Parliament continues to emphasise disclosure of interests rather than their avoidance, and with few exceptions, finds it unnecessary to restrict the outside employment of Members. The presumption of the propriety of holding outside financial interests is still predominant in the House. Furthermore, what some, mainly Labour, backbenchers regard as a most crucial area where financial interests can be abused remains outside the declaration requirements because the Government changed its mind about extending the declaration rule to Question Time. Arriving at the conclusion that this would involve practices which would be cumbersome and essentially time-wasting, a second motion on Members' Interests (Declaration) agreed to by the House on 12 July 1975 specifically laid down that for the purpose of the 1974 resolution the term 'proceeding' should not include the giving of any written notice or the asking of a supplementary question.

Contrary to the fears expressed by its opponents, the Register does not undermine the honour and self-restraint of the individual Member by removing his prerogative to be the sole judge of the relevancy of interests to be disclosed, nor does it necessarily signal the demise of mutual trust in the House. As recognised by the 1974 Select Committee on Members' Interests, 'in the end, responsibility must rest on the Member himself to disclose those interests that might affect his parliamentary actions' and the House trusts them in this respect (*HC* 102: 1974, para 10).

That the individual Member is still in practice the judge of the relevancy of interests which might affect his parliamentary action, and the fact that the Register cannot provide a guarantee against evasion, are crucial factors in an assessment of the extent to which the rule of declaration and the establishment of compulsory registration signify the erosion of a Member's privacy and indicate a move towards greater publicity. Combined with the shortcomings in the format of the Register discussed above, and the danger that registration becomes a replacement for, rather than supplementary to, the rule of disclosure, these facts point to the conclusion that both the contribution to increasing public knowledge of MPs' financial interests, and the concomitant erosion of a Member's privacy under the requirement of the Register, are less than the theory of registration would suggest. The difference is that Members wishing to safeguard their 'privacy' now positively have to be untruthful by making a 'nil' return in the Register instead of passively neglecting (forgetting) to make an affirmation in debate.

To these problems concerning the scope and format of the Register should be added one unintentional by-product of the Register. Paradoxically, by increasing public knowledge of MPs' interests the Register may also add to the risk of conflict or apparent conflict of interest arising. By providing a detailed catalogue of individual Member's interests, it actually helps public relations firms, companies etc. to identify which MPs might be useful to them.

The compulsory register of interests is in essence a *parliamentary* solution to the problem of conflict of interest, and as such retains the tradition of exclusive self-discipline by the House in the regulation of Members' interests. Investigation of the problem has been treated solely as a domestic matter and has been undertaken accordingly by a select committee of the House, not outside bodies. The Register was set up by a Resolution of the House, is monitored by a select committee of the House, and any refusal to comply with its procedures automatically becomes a matter for the House to resolve without interference from any other body except, indirectly from the media, whose efforts might in fact have a negative effect by promoting a closing of ranks.

6 The House of Commons and Internal Discipline

What problems arise out of the exclusive exercise of self-discipline in the regulation of Members' interests? A controversial issue is the propriety of the House acting as sole adjudicator upon the conduct of its Members in their parliamentary capacity. A practical consequence of this arrangement is the problem that at times the House is confronted with the difficult task of disciplining its own Members, with all the problems and personal loyalties which this involves. In this chapter we examine these issues against a background discussion of the procedures for investigation and punishment of misconduct available to the House.

Investigation

The House of Commons can choose between several procedures available for investigating allegations of misconduct against Members and Ministers, each more suitable for a particular type of inquiry and each subject to its own particular shortcomings.

Committee of Privileges

A formal complaint of breach of privilege – including misconduct by Members – must be raised in the House by a Member as soon as possible after the event which he is citing in the complaint occurs, and it is for the Speaker to pronounce whether this constitutes a *prima facie* breach of privilege. If he does so, it is usual for the Leader of the House to move a motion to refer the complaint to the Commons Select Committee of Privileges for investigation. This committee, comprising senior Members of the House, originated in the seventeenth century, and is a House of Commons not a Government committee. The House reserves for itself the final decision as to what action, if any, should be taken against the Member (or stranger). There is no obligation on the House to support the findings of the Committee of Privileges, even when it is unanimous. Partly because of the sensitivity of Members of Parliament to outside criticism and comments and partly because of the ease with which complaints may be raised, the Committee often finds itself dealing with trivial cases. This may to some extent account for the frequency, revealed by a survey of complaints referred to the Committee of Privileges since 1945[1], with which the Committee has recommended no further action, and the House has endorsed this recommendation. However, it should also be taken into account that many of the punishments available to the House are rarely thought appropriate for the present day.

Ad hoc select committees

Since the middle of the seventeenth century, for cases of alleged misconduct which raise issues besides that of privilege the House has often preferred to use *ad hoc* select committees. This preference was explained by the Rt. Hon. Winston Churchill when, as Prime Minister, he appointed a select committee in 1940 to investigate the conduct and activities of Mr. Robert Boothby MP in connection with the payment out of assets in Britain of claims against the Government of, and institutions in, the Republic of Czechoslovakia:

> I considered whether I should then move that it should be referred to the Committee of Privileges but, after obtaining guidance as to the precedents, I came to the conclusion that as the case appeared to raise other issues besides that of Privilege, it was better that it should go to a select committee, so that the truth could be ascertained and the conduct of the hon. Member considered. (*HC* 365: 1940, 829–831)

To some extent the thoroughness of this particular Committee, which found against Mr. Boothby and whose Report was agreed without division by the House, repaired the reputation of select committees as a method of inquiry. This had previously been badly discredited by the partisan proceedings of the select committee appointed to investigate the Marconi affair in 1913 (*HC* 351, 430,515,515–1: 1912 and 1913). That Committee had been set up to investigate allegations that Ministers in the Liberal Government had used their privileged knowledge of negotiations for a government contract with the Marconi company to speculate in Marconi shares. The Committee split along party lines and produced two reports. Its majority Report later gave rise to a similar split in the division lobbies after an acrimonious debate in the Commons. A Conservative motion for a vote of censure on the Ministers involved was rejected in favour of a Government motion which acquitted the Ministers of acting otherwise than in good faith, and reprobated charges of corruption brought against them which had been proved to be false.

The question of the efficacy of using *ad hoc* select committees for investigating alleged misconduct was again revived in the House in 1976, when a select committee was chosen as the appropriate instrument to inquire into the conduct and activities of Members of the House in connection with the affairs of Mr. J.G.L. Poulson (*HC* 490: 1977). This inquiry, which constitutes the most substantial parliamentary investigation of Members' conduct in recent times, concerned events which occurred *prior* to the establishment of the Register and the change of the convention of declaration of interests into a rule of the House. In reaching their judgment upon the conduct of Members the Committee therefore sought to apply the test that the House would have applied to its Members' conduct had it been aware of the facts at the time; namely the custom of declaration.

The Committee reported in July 1977 and, evoking some ill-defined standards concerning individual integrity and the reputation of the House found that the conduct of Mr. John Cordle (Cons) amounted to a contempt of the House, while that of Mr. Reginald Maudling (Cons) and Mr. Albert Roberts (Lab) was considered to have been inconsistent with the standards which the House was entitled to expect from its Members. Mr. Cordle resigned from the House on 22 July 1977. Four days later the House rejected Government proposals to agree with the Report's findings on Mr. Maudling and Mr. Roberts, in favour of supporting Conservative amendments simply to 'take note' of the Report in so far as it related to Maudling and Roberts. Mr. Edward Heath submitted that on this occasion the select committee had justified itself as a suitable means of dealing with allegations of misconduct. However, when Members passed through the division lobbies they were plainly split along party lines. In the vote on the Conservative 'take note' amendment relating to Mr. Maudling 210 of the 230 votes in favour were Conservative while 182 of the 207 cast against were Labour.

Tribunals of inquiry

As an alternative to inquiry by select committee, the House has in the past used special tribunals to remove controversial matters from the political sphere; for example, the 1888 Parnell Commission, the 1893

Featherstone Riots inquiry, and in 1915, the Dardanelles and Mesopotamia Commissions. Additionally, when allegations were made in 1921 against officials in the Ministry of Munitions, recent memories of the partisan failings of the select committee involved with the Marconi affair gave rise to demands for new investigatory machinery, not just for the munitions case, but for similar issues in the future.

The outcome was the Tribunals of Inquiry (Evidence) Act, 1921 providing, on a resolution of both Houses of Parliament, for a tribunal to inquire into definite matters of urgent public importance. The Act lays down no requirements as to the composition of the tribunal, but since 1948 the practice has been to appoint members of the judiciary and eminent QCs. This instrument of inquiry, the essence of which is the independence of the tribunal from the Executive and Parliament, is chiefly designed to investigate allegations of impropriety in public life. Examples of its use in relation to the Commons include the Budget disclosure inquiry in 1936 (Cmnd 5184:1936) and the Lynskey Tribunal in 1949 (Cmnd 7616:1949), both of which involved Government ministers, not backbenchers.

A number of important problems affecting the quasi-judicial procedure of tribunals have been identified[2] and the report of the tribunal investigating the Budget disclosure in 1936 itself drew attention to the difficulties facing both tribunal and witnesses, especially where the witness is a person whose conduct is in question. However, it is the fact that the prominent position of the Attorney General in these inquiries can be misconstrued that holds particular relevance for our discussion of conflict of interest. The role of leading counsel for the tribunal is usually played by the Attorney General. Here, as in giving advice and supplying information to select committees, the Attorney General represents the public interest. However, while he is expected to be the custodian of the public interest and to be politically impartial, he is also the chief law officer of the Crown, bound like the rest of his ministerial colleagues by collective ministerial responsibility. The advice he gives and the reasons behind his decisions are seldom if ever made public. If members of the Government in which the Attorney General holds office are directly involved in the allegations under inquiry the unfortunate conflicts of interest and loyalty that arise could result in the Attorney General's impartiality being questioned and the public interest appearing to be compromised for partisan advantage.

Penal Jurisdiction of the House

Although a select committee or tribunal report may be condemnatory of the conduct of a Member or Minister, it is for the House as a whole, as sole judge of its own proceedings, to decide what action, if any, to take on those findings. Deriving from the medieval conception of Parliament primarily as a Court of Justice, the House has a range of sanctions at its disposal if it decides that a Member or non-member is guilty of a breach of privilege or an unspecified contempt of Parliament, some of which, though used to effect in parliamentary history, are rarely countenanced in present circumstances. With regard to the disciplining of its own Members, these sanctions are listed in *Erskine May* 19 ed. as follows: the power of commitment, which May describes as the 'keystone of parliamentary privilege', but which has not been exercised by the Commons since 1880 (*CJ* [1880] 77, 235); expulsion or suspension from the service of the House; and reprimand or admonition administered by the Speaker. Earlier in history the Commons had the additional right to impose fines but this right has not been exercised since 1666 (*CJ* [1660–70] 690), and as remarked by the Clerk of the House in his memorandum to the Committee of Privileges in 1977 (*HC* 417: 1977), the doubt as to whether the House of Commons, in contrast to the House of Lords, is a court of record implies the further doubt as to whether they now possess this power.

The House: prosecutor and judge?

As we discovered in chapter 4, the claim to be the sole judge over both its Members and proceedings derives in part from the origins of Parliament as the High Court of Parliament, the highest court in the land, and the belief that it would therefore be contrary to every principle for its proceedings to be regulated or challenged in any other court. However, this view has been challenged by critics who consider the arrangement whereby Parliament is both prosecutor and judge in its own cause offends against the principles of natural justice, and who find the rights of the Commons too indefinite, uncertain and in many cases archaic.

This argument was cogently put to the Select Committee on Parliamentary Privilege, which was set up in 1967 amid increasing concern at the sensitivity of Members to outside criticism, to conduct a general review of the law of parliamentary privilege (*HC* 34: 1977). In their memorandum of evidence to this Committee, the Study of Parliament Group[3] criticised the indefinite scope of the House's powers of privilege and contempt, arguing:

> The result of this undefined reach of the House's powers whether by way of contempt or applications of privilege is to maintain uncertainty about a large number of activities occuring outside the House which affect Members in their roles as public representatives. The development of different modes of opinion

formation, interest group activity and political organisation inside and outside Parliament has obviously altered in a radical way the pressures which operate upon Members and the environment in which they carry out their duties. Yet Privilege rests in part on eighteenth-century assumptions. (*HC* 34: 1977, 189–90)

Although not claiming originality for the suggestion, they also recommended a possible transfer of the House's power of punishment for contempt or breach of privilege to a more appropriate forum for adjudication. In their opinion, whatever its formal status, an assembly comprising six hundred and thirty Members is unsuitable for conducting the essentially adjudicative process of resolving individual cases arising under the law and custom of Parliament. Just as the House had been persuaded of the wisdom of committing to courts the adjudication of disputed elections (by the Parliamentary Elections Act, 1868) so, they suggested, consideration should now be given to a similar transfer to the courts of jurisdiction over cases of contempt or breach of privilege:

> We think that there are good reasons both for clarifying the scope of privilege and contempt powers in principle and also for providing a judicial forum where justice is seen to be done in individual cases. It is reasonable that citizens and political interests of all kinds should know what they may and may not do and the situation of uncertainty which indefinite powers engender seems unhealthy whatever its historical justification. (Ibid p. 195)

This is a controversial view which is opposed not just on historical grounds but also because of the practical problems involved in its implementation. Mr. L.A. Abraham, a former Principal Clerk of Committees in the House of Commons expressed this belief to the 1967 Privilege Committee, who themselves found against transferring the penal jurisdiction of the House to some other tribunal:

> If . . . the jurisdiction over contempts of the House of Commons were transferred from the House to the courts, it would be necessary to enumerate the acts and omissions which were to constitute criminal offences in the statute by which the jurisdiction was so transferred – a task to the difficulty of which anyone who has helped to draft or advise upon Power-and-Privileges-of-Parliament Acts for the new Commonwealth countries can bear witness. (Ibid p. 106)

Recalling the House's preference for indefiniteness, flexibility and discretion in its rules and procedures, it is interesting to note that similar arguments were raised against establishing a register of Members' interests by statute; a move which would have involved the task, which some MPs thought intractable, of defining comprehensively and fairly in law what interests were to be registered by Members.

An aspect of the debate as to whether the House should abandon its jurisdiction to punish for contempt or breach of privilege that has particular relevance for us is whether MPs can, and should be, brought within the criminal law on corruption[4] for activities in their parliamentary capacity. For although we have seen that the situation of conflict of interest is not synonymous with the act of corruption, we have also established that corruption is a possible solution to this conflict, whereby personal financial interest overcomes or distorts the exercise of an official's public duties and responsibilities.

The common belief that only the House of Commons and not the criminal courts can deal with a corrupt Member acting in his parliamentary capacity was dogmatically upheld by the Salmon Commission. They reasoned that unlike a Minister of the Crown who is holder of a public office and could be dealt with under common law for corrupt activity in connection with his ministerial duties, neither the statutory nor the common law applied to the bribery or attempted bribery of a Member of Parliament in respect of his parliamentary activities. Explaining why this is so they stated:

> It is clear to us that a Member of Parliament cannot, in that capacity, be deemed an 'agent' for the purpose of the Prevention of Corruption Act 1906. It is equally clear that Parliament could not be deemed to be a 'public body' for the purposes of the Public Bodies Corrupt Practices Act of 1889. Nor does membership of Parliament, as such, constitute public office for the purposes of the common law. (Cmnd 6524:1976, para 307)

This view was also upheld by a former Prime Minister, the Rt. Hon. James Callaghan, when asked in October 1976 in the wake of the Poulson affair, to clarify the position in law of MPs in relation to allegations of corruption (*HC Debs* 917:1976, 1446). Thus the image is unintentionally created of Members of Parliament being above the law (though subject to the law of Parliament) and the danger arises of the media and the public thinking that double standards are being applied by the House.

While in no way questioning the right of the House to govern its own procedures, the Salmon Commission nevertheless felt that the sanctions against bribery introduced by the criminal law in other fields had outstripped the sanctions now available to Parliament. As already stated, the power of commitment has not been exercised by the Commons since 1880, and the right to impose fines has not been exercised since 1666. This leaves the House with the penalties of reprimand or admonition administered by the Speaker, and expulsion or suspension from the services of the House. Use of the latter two options was argued against by Mr. Michael Foot and Sir Derek Walker-Smith in the debate on the conduct of Members in 1977 on the grounds that they impose a penalty not only on the Member but also on his constituents (*HC Debs* 936: 1977, 348 and 419). However, the manifest purpose of expulsion is remedial rather than disciplinary: to rid the House of an MP considered by the House collectively as unfit for membership (*Erskine May* 19 ed., p. 132). This does not prevent the expelled MP from serving again in Parliament if he is re-elected. Thus expulsion – but not suspension – does not deprive the electors of their representative, but actually gives them the chance to reconsider, in the light of his conduct, whether the Member is someone who should represent them. It is doubtful, however, whether constituents would necessarily pass judgment on the conduct of a Member in the ensuing by-election; party loyalty or current economic interests may weigh heavier in their scale of priorities.

Believing these penalties the House may impose to be inappropriate to present circumstances, the Select Committee of Privileges in 1967 (*HC* 34) and again in 1977 (*HC* 417) recommended that legislation should be introduced to revive the power of the House to impose fines. Along with most of the other recommendations contained in the 1967 Privileges Report this suggestion has not been implemented. In the context of seeking a suitable sanction for Members who refuse to register their interests, the revival of fines could be commended as a more suitable punishment by the House than either suspension or expulsion. Although we might then find situations in which fines were paid by the outside interest which was the subject of the offence, this would probably be treated as a contempt.

Commenting solely on the adequacy of sanctions for punishing bribery and corruption, the Salmon Commission recommended that 'Parliament should consider bringing corruption, bribery and attempted bribery of a Member of Parliament acting in his parliamentary capacity within the ambit of the criminal law (Cmnd 6524:1976, para 311). The decision on whether to implement or even discuss this recommendation inevitably remains with Parliament. As yet, the House of Commons has not discussed the Report, although it was debated in the House of Lords on 8 December 1976. An even stronger case can be made for advocating that Ministers, custodians of the public purse, should be subject to the 'law of the land', not only in the performance of ministerial duties but also in their parliamentary capacity.

However, taking the criminal law on corruption as it stands, it is possible to argue along lines pursued by Dr. Geoffrey Marshall[5] that there is in fact no 'bizarre loophole' which allows MPs to escape prosecution when they are acting in their parliamentary capacity. This view has been developed by Graham Zellick who argues against the Royal Commission's assessment and constructs a strong case for asserting that the criminal law can as it stands operate in this area.[6] The nub of his argument is as follows. First he considers it is not at all clear that the House of Commons could not be deemed to be a 'public body' for the purposes of the Public Bodies Corrupt Practices Act, 1889. Then, turning to common law which punishes bribery and breach of trust by public officers, he asks whether membership of Parliament can constitute 'public office' for this purpose. No prosecutions have been brought in England because the House has consistently treated corruption of Members as a contempt of the House. However, he is able to point to judgments in the High Court and State courts in Australia, where it has been held that membership of Parliament is a public office for the purposes of criminal law,[7] and accordingly payments to an MP in connection with his parliamentary work could amount to common law misdemeanours. In some of these judgments a broader basis of liability has been favoured stretching to all persons whatever holding offices of 'public trust and confidence'. For example, in *R v Boston*, Higgins J. took the view that:

> . . . it seems to me immaterial whether the member is to be treated as a public officer or not. He is a member of Parliament, holding a fiduciary relation towards the public, and that is enough.[8]

Thus, on one ground or another, Zellick considers Members of Parliament would seem to be caught by the common law. Summing up his argument he concludes:

> It must be recorded that there is a distinct possibility that the acceptance of payments by Members of Parliament in certain circumstances, hitherto thought to lie within the exclusive cognisance of Parliament, may constitute criminal offences, which the House could instruct the Attorney-General to prosecute, Article 9 of the Bill of Rights notwithstanding.[9]

Zellick has plainly shown that the existing law is not so clear cut as the Royal Commission believed. The traditional view that only the House can deal with corruption of and by its Members is overdue for review. It has its roots in the ancient law of Parliament, but the various privileges embodied in this law should not themselves be immune from review in the light of changing historical circumstances. Clarification in this area would be beneficial to MPs themselves who, if the impression gained from my sample survey of MPs is correct, tend to be confused or uninformed themselves both as to the distinction between conflict of interest and corruption, and as to their position in law relating to allegations of corruption.

Self-Discipline: Practical Problems

The Clerk to the 1977 Select Committee on Conduct of Members (*HC* 409) stated that 'the privilege of immunity from outside investigation of proceedings in Parliament carries with it the corollary that the House should always, if the occasion arises, be prepared to do this job for itself'.[10] Unfortunately, parliamentary self-discipline, buttressed by tradition though it be, has allowed the House to be open to charges of partisan political motives or alternatively of acting defensively with *esprit de corps* in the manner of a gentlemen's club when charges are brought against any of the body.

The Marconi inquiry discussed above amply illustrates the potential for partisan political motivation and the closing of ranks which can surround a select committee inquiry into alleged misconduct. Recognising this the Royal Commission on Tribunals of Inquiry in 1966 aknowledged the usefulness of select committees for many purposes but was adamant that because of the likelihood of real or apparent political bias 'the investigation of allegations of public misconduct is not one of them' (Cmnd 3121:1966, para 35). It warned that to go back to such procedure would be a retrograde step. Nevertheless, as we have seen, the House is keen to retain the doctrine that decisions on the standards of conduct of hon. Members can never be handed over to an outside body and continues to favour *ad hoc* select committees to investigate allegations of misconduct.

During the debate in 1977 on the conduct of Messrs. Maudling and Roberts in connection with Mr. Poulson, Mr. George Strauss, then Father of the House, warned against the danger of institutional loyalty and club spirit in dealing with alleged misconduct. He argued:

> We must . . . avoid the feeling that someone who has misbehaved or done something that he should not have done may get special treatment or sympathy because he is liked or has done great service to Parliament . . . We must not refrain from action because of the old school tie, or for any other reason. (*HC Debs* 936:1977, 367).

Mr. Strauss himself did not refrain from action. He tabled an amendment for the suspension of both Mr. Maudling and Mr. Roberts from sitting in the House of Commons for six months. The amendment failed; as we have seen Maudling and Roberts were in effect cleared of criticism on a 'take note' motion, and it was Mr. Strauss himself who risked censure in the form of an Early Day Motion tabled by members of the Opposition, expressing no confidence in the Father of the House.

On this occasion personal factors, set within their inevitable framework of party politics were at play again. It is likely that the intervention of Mr. Heath who effectively gave his word, as former Prime Minister, for the truth, accuracy and frankness of Mr. Maudling as a minister of the Crown aroused considerable sympathy for Mr. Maudling in the House. It is equally likely, as Mr. Michael Alison observed, that the fact that Mr. John Cordle was perhaps 'not universally popular or one of the great figures or personalities of the House' attributed to the pressure, unjust in Mr. Alison's opinion, for his resignation (*HC Debs* 936:1977, 402–3). In contrast to a show of institutional loyalty, in Mr. Cordle's case Mr. Alison believed that the House had borne out Mr. Michael Foot's fear, expressed earlier in the debate, that on occasions the House can operate 'a liberal form of lynch law' imposed by a 'sanctimonious mob'.

Personal factors are undoubtedly important in determining the penalty for alleged misconduct. For further illustration of this we can refer to the investigation into the conduct of Robert Boothby in 1940, cited above. Following the acceptance by the House of a condemnatory Select Committee Report, Boothby resigned from ministerial office (but remained as a backbench MP). His memoirs, which like any other memoirs have to be read with caution, claim that Churchill was 'out for the kill' and cite Lloyd George as saying to Boothby, 'if I had been there, this would never have happened'.[11] Sir John Colville attempted to exonerate Churchill from the charge of hounding Boothby out of office, but in doing so he reveals the antipathy of the Tory Chief Whip and others who had demanded that Boothby should actually be impeached.[12] The political career of Robert – later Lord – Boothby also illustrates the point that agreement by the House with a critical report from a select committee or tribunal does not necessarily foreshadow the end of a political career.

Enforcing the Register: The Enoch Powell Case

A compulsory register of interests implies sanctions and the House has encountered serious difficulties in disciplining Members who refuse to comply with the registration requirement. A main preoccupation of the Select Committee on Members' Interests has been the failure of Mr. Enoch Powell to register his interests.

In March 1976 on behalf of the Committee, the Registrar of Members' Interests had written to Mr. Powell asking him to explain why he had not complied with the Order of 22 May 1974. In reply Mr. Powell had referred the Registrar to his letter of 1 July 1975, in which he had alluded to his speech in the House on 12 June 1975 when he had argued that the Orders, not having been imposed by legislation, were unconstitutional. Before examining the reaction of the Select

Committee, it is interesting to examine more closely Mr. Powell's reasons for refusing to comply with the Register.

During an interview for the research on which this study is based, he elaborated on the two main reasons which he had given during the debate on 12 June: namely that the Register was degrading to the House and, more importantly, that it was unconstitutional. Mr. Powell insisted that he could have offered several arguments against the resolution even if it had been constitutional, but he felt that he had to be careful not to argue these reasons at length or to give them too much emphasis because that would detract from the likelihood of his constitutional position being understood.

He stressed that his 'protest' position, which rested on the grounds that the Register was unlawful and unconstitutional, was in a way separate from and independent of the reservations which he would have supposing the resolution was constitutional. The nub of his argument was that the House was imposing by resolution a new qualification for Membership, namely having to make a return in the Register, if they wanted to sit and vote and speak as Members of Parliament. This, he said, was unconstitutional because the House could not by its own resolution alter the conditions of Membership. This was a confusion between the effect of a resolution of the House, which is internal to the House, and legislation, which changes the law of the land and in which the House only participates. He argued that the fact that the original Select Committee on Members' Interests (Declaration) in 1974 had found themselves led to consider the inclusion of parliamentary candidates, and particularly the unfairness in the case of an election at which the ex-Member who was standing had to declare his interests while the other candidates were under no obligations to disclose anything, lent support to his argument that the resolution of the House attempted to alter the law of the land and not just to regulate procedure of the House.

He pointed out that there was an 'unresolvable paradox' in his position. On the one hand, he was saying that the House of Commons has the right as the House of Commons to pass any resolution and to punish any Member either for disobedience or for no cause shown. This position asserts the unrestricted power of the House of Commons over its Members on the grounds that 'you cannot uphold the sovereignty of Parliament unless you accord to each House of Parliament unlimited power'. Here he means unlimited in the sense of not being limited by the possibility of appeal to any other authority. There is an appeal – in a metaphorical sense – to the electorate. But this appeal is only indirect; if the electorate so wish they can make nonsense of the House's right to expel a Member by repeatedly re-electing him as in the case of John Wilkes.[13] From this position of the unlimited jurisdiction of the House over its own Members, he would agree that the House could expel him for not complying with the resolution, whether or not his constitutional contention was correct.

On the other hand, he was asserting that the House of Commons was attempting to do something that it could not do without 'betraying its own essence'. In his words, 'you cannot, as maker and upholder of the law, purport to make law in a way that law cannot be made'. He was, he said, in 'the classic position of a person who disobeys in the name of a higher right while fully acknowledging the authority which he disobeys'. He likened his position to that of Thomas More who, in 1534, refused to accept King Henry VIII's supremacy over the Church. More did not dispute the omnicompetence of Parliament but would not obey because it was doing something which judged from another standpoint it could not do. More's proposition related to the universal Church and its nature, while he was faced with a conflict between, on the one hand, the right of the House to enforce upon its Members any resolutions that it pleases, and on the other hand, the right of all citizens to live under the rule of the law, and more specifically, in this case, to have the conditions and qualifications for membership of the House of Commons determined and fixed by the law. He held that this conflict of right, and the associated conflict of loyalty – conflict between the loyalty that a Member owes to the House and that which is owed to the constitution – can be resolved only from the standpoint of the constitution, viz. that the conditions and qualifications for Membership of the House must be determined and fixed by the law. Mr. Powell added that his objective was different from More's. Whereas More objected on grounds related to the content of the Act, his objection was irrespective of the wisdom or otherwise of the resolution. He saw no solution to the paradox. He insisted that he would not consent to making a return in the Register, whatever the consequences. Whether the House should or could as a matter of practicality punish him, he saw as another issue; but he agreed that, if it wished, the House did have the power to punish him.

The Select Committee on Members' Interests acknowledged that the House might consider Mr. Powell's refusal a contempt, but thinking it more satisfactory if the House made general provision by exercising its right to regulate its own proceedings in a way which would be binding on all Members, they recommended the House adopt a standing order which would provide for the suspension of a Member who failed to register his interests wholly or in part (*HC* 479: 1976). Frustrated by the Government's unwillingness to provide time to debate their Report recommending this proposal, they issued a Special Report in December 1976 (*HC* 84) informing the House that they were not prepared to commend a further edition of the Register (now in its second edition –

HC 284: 1976) until the House had expressed a view on the force of its original disclosure resolutions. In effect, the Committee, no doubt embarrassed by Mr. Powell's notification of his refusal to comply with the resolutions, had decided to meet the Government's failure to allow the House time to reach a decision on the enforcement of its original resolutions by going on strike. Although their action prevented the publication for sale of further annual editions of the Register for the remainder of that Parliament, without abrogating a resolution of the House they could not prevent the Register from being compiled and maintained. Thus, the Registrar continued to keep an up-to-date manuscript edition of the Register in his office, where it remained open for public inspection, and in the House of Commons library for consultation by Members.

The matter remained unresolved when Parliament was dissolved in April 1979. Shortly after the new Parliament assembled the remaining manuscript copies of the Register were withdrawn on the grounds that they contained information on persons no longer Members. The Registrar was obliged by the Resolutions of 1974 and 1975 to send out the declaration forms to all MPs and produce a master copy of the Register within a month of the new Parliament, but until the Conservative Government set up a new Select Committee on Members' Interests he had no authority to publish it. The new Select Committee was finally set up in November 1979 and, while still upholding the opinions of its predecessor Committee, eventually decided to go ahead and allow publication of a new Register and then deal with actions against Members who refused to comply, who now totalled five.[14] A new edition of the Register was published accordingly on 5 June 1980 (*HC* 617) and further editions have been published yearly.[15]

To date no action has been taken against Members who refuse to comply with the Register. When asked by the author why the 1976 Report from the Select Committee on Members' Interests had never been debated, Mr. Michael Foot, then Leader of the House, pointed out that whereas in 1974 there had been a temporary legislative void which could be filled by the introduction of the Register, by 1976 the political climate had changed. The parliamentary session was busy and could not accommodate the new issues relating to the Register. He referred to two particular time-consuming issues on the parliamentary agenda during this period: first, public policy deriving from the Government's economic and social measures and magnified by the controversy deriving from the devolution issue; second, the pressure of 'Members' matters', i.e. pay, pensions etc., which were jostling for attention and which had to be debated, in the main, late at night. To have resolved the matter of Enoch Powell's refusal to register would, in Mr. Foot's view, have taken up much of this valuable time. As a strong upholder of parliamentary procedures and traditions, he did not think it right that the House should take lightly a matter involving the possible censure of a Member. The fact that during this period Mr. Powell's vote, and the support he had among the UUUC Members, had been crucial for the Labour Government may also have contributed to the Government's unwillingness to debate the matter.

Mr. Powell himself suggested an altogether different reason why the issue of non-compliance, raised by his own refusal, has not been resolved. Begging the fundamental problem discussed earlier of what constitutes an 'interest' in politics, he argued that he had an 'unfair advantage' in that the House knew that he had no interests influencing his parliamentary behaviour. Talking in 1979, he considered his success, which he then construed as the achievement of destroying the 1974 resolution concerning registration by his single act of defiance, would not have been possible without this extraneous advantage. It contributed to the impracticability of the House enforcing its resolutions because they would have had to censure a Member whom everyone knows has 'no interests' and would not be influenced by them even if he had, and who is a zealous upholder of the sovereignty, rules and procedures of the House. Thus, he concluded that extraneous factors, in his case his 'unfair advantage', are often as important or more important than the validity of the case.

My review of the practical problems of parliamentary self-discipline suggests the general conclusion that it is indeed extraneous factors – partisan political motivation, club spirit, personal factors for example – which are frequently as important or more important in the disciplining of Members than the validity of the case.

7 Multiple Standards?

First, we must consider our own position rather than that of other people. The first step should be to put our own house in order. (Mr. Prior, Lord President, *HC Debs* 865:1973, 23)

The emphasis on parliamentary *self*-discipline has led some critics to question whether the House of Commons has been as vigilant in putting its own house in order as it has been in making or recommending the standards for other public servants to keep. Successive Governments have argued in defence that functional differences between the House and other institutions engaged in the public service account for different degrees of stringency in the regulation of pecuniary interests. In chapter 4 we encountered the strict code of conduct for Ministers in the form of written guidance from the Prime Minister. In this chapter we go outside the precincts of Westminster and observe the rules of conduct operating in neighbouring Whitehall, and the more parochial territories of local government.

Two official Reports provide the background material for this broader perspective. The Redcliffe-Maud Report (Cmnd 5636:1974) was the product of a Prime Minister's Committee on Local Government Rules of Conduct. Set up by Mr. Heath in October 1973 it was given the brief:

To examine present local government law and practice as it relates to or might affect: (i) the conduct of both members and officers in situations where there is or could be a conflict between their positions in local government and their private interests.

(ii) qualification or disqualification for service as a member of a local authority or any of its committees. To consider the adequacy of the operation of such law and practice and the principles which should apply, and make recommendations regarding compliance with such principles.

This Committee reported in May 1974 and soon after, the new Labour Government appointed the Royal Commission on Standards of Conduct in Public Life (Cmnd 6524:1976). The task of the Salmon Commission was to

> . . . inquire into standards of conduct in central and local government and other public bodies in the United Kingdom in relation to the problems of conflict of interest and the risk of corruption involving favourable treatment from a public body; and to make recommendations as to the future safeguards which may be required to ensure the highest standard of probity in public life.

Both inquiries were set up in response to public anxiety caused by the Poulson affair.

The Civil Service

While our interest lies with contemporary arrangements, we should not forget that the concept of a civil service as a body of impartial experts in administration serving the nation irrespective of their own gain is a fairly recent phenomenon. As E.N. Gladden observed:

> It was not until the defeat of patronage and the introduction of impartial selection by means of open competition that the ideal of a profession, impartial and devoted service to the State, irrespective of the political colour of the Government took on its modern shape.[1]

Changes in the selection, organisation and training of the home civil service in the second half of the nineteenth century laid the foundations for the current arrangements for ensuring ethical conduct, arrangements which a former General Secretary of the First Division Association of Civil Servants recommended to me as a model for the rest of the public sector. What does this model comprise?

Legal safeguards

There is no comprehensive civil service statute in Britain as under many modern systems of Government. However, two particular statutes do have a bearing on standards of conduct in the civil service. Firstly, civil servants are covered by the controversial *Official Secrets Acts* of 1911 and 1920, which impose penalties for the disclosure of information. It is an offence for a civil servant to disclose, without first obtaining permission, to any unauthorised person any information which has been acquired during his official duties unless the information has already been made public. The Acts extend to non-secret as well as secret information and remain in force after the official has retired or left the civil service. Secondly, as we discovered in chapter 2, civil servants are covered by the Prevention of Corruption Act, 1906, althought not the Public Bodies Corrupt Practices Act, 1889.

Code of Conduct

In the absence of a civil service statute, the terms and conditions of service are governed by the Minister for the Civil Service (the Prime Minister) by Prerogative Orders in Council.[2] The detail and operation of the general powers provided by the Orders are contained in minutes and circulars made under the Order. Originally authority to regulate the civil service in this way lay with the Treasury, but passed to the newly established Civil Service Department in 1968. When this was wound up in 1979, responsibility for standards of conduct was transferred to an Office of Management and Personnel, housed in the Cabinet Office.

These minutes and circulars were not codified into any single document until 1944, when consolidation of principle took place in the form of a Treasury document known as 'Estacode'. This provided civil servants with a number of broad principles of conduct, including the instruction to avoid a conflict between duty and private interest. Since around 1975 the contents of 'Estacode' have been split into two separate documents: the Civil Service Pay and Conditions of Service Code (hereafter referred to as the Code), and the Establishment Officers Guide (hereafter referred to as the Guide).

The Code broadly reflects the principles of 'Estacode' and includes instructions from two sources: from relevant legislation, and from agreements reached in negotiation with the National Staff Side of the Whitley Council or with Staff Associations themselves direct (the National Staff Side being a federation of nine independent civil service trade unions). The Code sets out general principles of conduct which refer to exceptional standards of service, personal honesty, integrity and impartiality, and which urge civil servants to avoid situations where their duty and private interests may be seen to conflict. It also provides guidance on the acceptance of gifts and rewards. In general, 'an officer must not, either directly or indirectly accept any gift, reward or benefit from any member of the public or organisation with whom he has been brought into contact by reason of his official duties'.[3] The civil servant is also reminded of his responsibilities with regard to the disclosure of official information and is given advice on activities involving the use of official information or experience.

The rules are issued as guidance but are mandatory on employing departments. Some rules have a specifically defined method of application, for others the principles are stated and the method of application left to the discretion of the individual department. The Guide is provided for use by the personnel services and administrative services in Government departments and is broadly speaking an aid in interpreting the Code; for example, it contains additional guidance on the exercise of departmental discretion. Unlike the Code, it is not available to employees.

Departmental rules

Within the civil service the emphasis, as far as possible, is on delegating responsibility for rules of conduct to employing departments. The civil servant, therefore, has to familiarise himself with the rules of his own department as well as the general requirements of the central Code. Infringements of these administrative rules are dealt with under the civil service's own disciplinary machinery.

In part, departmental rules provide instructions common to all departments. For example, each civil servant is requested to consult with his Establishment Officer if he intends to retain or acquire a shareholding which might conceivably conflict with the interests of his department. He is also required to disclose the fact if he comes into contact in his official capacity with any business or commercial organisation in which he has a private interest. Thus, whereas for a local government officer it is a criminal offence under section 117 of the Local Government Act, 1972 to fail to disclose a pecuniary interest, for a civil servant it only constitutes infringement of departmental rules and is an in-service disciplinary matter.

Departmental rules also provide specific guidance on outside interests or activities judged to be incompatible with employment in that particular department. Examined historically the civil service existed as a group of independent departments. Although a measure of common regulation and staffing policy has gradually developed, it is still better understood as a diverse entity rather than a homogenous institution. Different departments perform varied functions and have differing levels of contact with the private sector. Once this is recognised, the need for departments to have flexibility in formulating staff rules for their specific circumstances can be appreciated. The Salmon Commission recognised, for example, that standards of conduct become more ambiguous and the opportunities for corruption increase at the interface between the public sector and the private sector. As the comments of a former Managing Director of a Glasgow engineering firm (jailed on eight charges of corruption) illustrate, the habits and customs of profit-making business concerns may be at odds with those expected in public life. Asked on television[4] whether he could have operated his business without bribing people, Maurice Cochran claimed, 'no way, no way . . . we would have gone to the wall'. He said that bribery was normal to commercial business and that it struck him as odd that he was even being asked questions about it. It is not surprising, therefore, that the Staff Rules of the Department of Environment specifically advise employees:

> . . . the nature of the Department's activities often calls for a close working relationship with commercial organisations and whilst it is in no way implied that staff of contractors with whom the Department has dealings are likely to act improperly in such circumstances, it must be recognised that by virtue of their position, staff involved in the placing, supervision or overall control of contracts could be particularly vulnerable to criticism. Certain rules therefore exist to safeguard the interests of the staff concerned.[5]

Pantouflage

Interaction between the public sector and the private sector is also the root cause of concern surrounding the employment opportunities for civil servants upon resignation or retirement. Senior civil servants may be criticised of being out of touch with the world outside Whitehall, but it remains a fact that they have shown themselves to be exceptionally marketable to business and industry. Subject to certain safeguards, it has never been the general practice to discourage civil servants from taking up business appointments on leaving the public service. On the contrary, in 1975 the then Prime Minister (Harold Wilson) publicly stated that he believed,

> It is very much in the public interest that people with experience of public administration in the Crown Service should, in suitable cases, be able to move into business and industry, where their experience and their qualities may be of great value. (*HC Debs* 894:1975, 495–6)

However, the smooth operation of this arrangement breaks down when there are suspicions that a particular appointment is improper. Scope for suspicion has increased with the development of a new form of patronage by senior civil servants, who can appoint people to quangos and public sector boards. Rules exist, therefore, to safeguard against situations where a serving officer might be suspected of favouring a particular company or organisation in order to secure future lucrative employment, or where an organisation might be thought to have an improper advantage over its competitors by recruiting a former civil servant who, in the course of his public service career, may have been party to information considered 'trade secrets' by these competitors.

These rules were established in 1937 following a case where the permanent secretary of a Government department had discussed with the board of a company the possibility of future employment with them, while at the same time officially negotiating with the company over a Government contract. Modified from time to time, their current effect can be summarised as follows. Officers of the rank of under-secretary and above and of the equivalent rank in the armed forces are obliged to obtain permission from the Government before accepting, within two years of resignation or retirement, outside appointments with firms which have close contractual or financial connections with the Government. Since 1975 permanent secretaries have also been barred for three months on leaving the service from taking up outside commercial appointments, unless the Prime Minister gives an individual dispensation on the grounds that the national interest is overriding.

In practice, individual cases involving permanent secretaries and second permanent secretaries (except where the intended employment is with a non-commercial body) are referred to a standing advisory committee headed by the former Labour Treasury Minister, Lord Diamond. This committee assists the Prime Minister, who makes the final decision. Other cases involving lower grades are usually left for the discretion of the Minister heading the department in which the officer concerned is employed. To give some indication of the scale of these procedures, between 1973 and 1980 out of a total of 514 applications covered by the criteria, nine were not approved and 71 were permitted with conditions. The rest were approved without any conditions.[6]

The rules are primarily intended to reassure the public about the impartiality of state servants. They are designed not simply to avoid the risk of actual temptation or corruption, but to avoid even the suspicion of conflict of interest. They go beyond what is required of the civil servant in law and also beyond what is required of Government Ministers. As we saw in chapter 4 the written guidance to ministers does not extend to former ministers taking employment (for example, directorships) or acquiring interests on leaving Office. Nevertheless, controversy surrounding senior public officials taking jobs in business has occurred. Criticism of the practice gathered momentum in 1975, when the late Lord Armstrong took early retirement to become chairman of the Midland Bank shortly after resigning as head of the home civil service. There has since been a steady stream of retired civil servants taking jobs in industry or commerce. Better known appointments include those of Sir Antony Part, former permanent secretary at the Department of Industry, who became a non-executive director of Lucas, EMI, Metal Box and Debenhams among other organisations, and Lord Hunt, former Cabinet Secretary, who within a few months of retirement became chairman of the London subsidiary of the Banque Nationale de Paris, the nationalised French bank. The transfer from public to private sector did not go so smoothly for Sir Freddie Kearns, former second permanent secretary at the Ministry of Agriculture, who was reportedly blocked by the Prime Minister from joining the National Farmers' Union as a consultant until a year had elapsed after his retirement.

With growing unease over the movement of former civil servants into business and industry the rules, as well as the practice of what the French refer to as *pantouflage*, have come under fire. In 1981 the Commons Treasury and Civil Service Committee conducted a review of the acceptance of outside appointments by Crown servants. This all-party Commons Committee was critical of existing procedures which they believed 'tilted too much in the direction of freedom of movement and too little in the direction of removing the suspicion of impropriety'.[7] They condemned the existing rules as being too vague, inconsistently applied and too closely controlled by civil servants. One of the Committee members, a Conservative MP, is on record as speaking of 'subliminal corruption' of officials in the final years of their public service career, coming to accept that when they retire they get 'a clutch of highly paid, highly prestigious appointments'.[8]

The Committee's proposals for stricter and less secretive rules were roundly opposed by the Council of Civil Service Unions, who found particularly objectionable the implication that senior civil servants could not be expected to play fair unless the existing code of conduct were enforceable with legal sanctions. The rules remain unchanged but growing parliamentary concern prompted an all-party subcommittee of the Treasury and Civil Service Committee to review the procedures once again. Their report has not yet been officially published (August 1984) but the *Observer* (8.7.1984) carried details of its contents, which have been leaked. It seems the Committee is to recommend firmer controls, increasing from two to five years the period of time following resignation or retirement during which a civil servant may be prevented from accepting a job in the private sector, and introducing sanctions – including the loss of a substantial inflation-proof pension – for violation of these controls. They are also likely to recommend establishing a new 'oversight' committee to produce regular reports on the movement of senior Whitehall advisors into industry. It remains to be seen whether any of these proposals will be implemented by a Government which is keen both to promote the interchange between the public and private sectors, and to maintain integrity in the civil service.

'Culture conflict'

Problems arising from interaction between the public sector and the private sector are not restricted to personnel movement in one direction. Just as the transfer of public servants into the private sector can attract criticism, an influx of temporary civil servants on short-term and contract appointments presents a different set of problems. In discussing departmental rules we touched on the potential culture conflict between the habits and customs of the commercial world and those expected in public life. A former General Secretary of the First Division Association of Civil Servants confirmed this problem and suggested to me that uncertainties concerning proper conduct were more common with temporary civil servants, who are less likely to become acclimatised to the civil service norms and mores of integrity and impartiality than 'established' career civil servants. This view had earlier been canvassed internally by the Society of Civil Servants, who at the time of the Salmon inquiry saw no need for tightening up the rules of conduct of the civil service, but argued:

> Where there is a potential danger is in the growing practice of making direct outside appointments, either permanently or on a contract basis. When people enter the Service relatively late in life, they come in with a background, ethos and standards which may well be quite different from those of the Service. A redundant sales manager or purchasing manager, or someone from a merchant bank or finance House, who enters as a direct entry principal will take for granted practices and customs which are foreign to our (rightly) relatively puritanical traditions.[9]

Unwritten ethic

This really brings us to the heart of the civil service model for ensuring ethical conduct – a professional ethic which is presumed to become part of the make-up of each civil servant:

> . . . the ethic is that we stand committed to neutrality of process . . . public power is not to be used to further the private purposes of those to whom it is entrusted . . . it is to be used solely for the furtherance of public purpose as defined by constitutional process.[10]

All the formal rules we have discussed so far are constructed upon the foundation of this unwritten code of ethics. A crucial question therefore is how sound does this foundation remain in a situation of increasing interaction between Whitehall and industry, and where regard must be paid to the fluidity and changes occurring in the relationship between civil servants and ministers. The professional ethic may have validity as a universal principle in the public service, but the difficulty increasingly lies in its practical application.

Local Government

> . . . most serious crime has centred around planning decisions and local government housing and development contracts. (para 37)
>
> The conditions created by Parliament in the field of planning law and in urban housing development have put greater strain than has been generally realised upon our system of locally elected council . . . . (para 38)

Thus the Salmon Commission alluded to the incentives and pressures to corruption within local government. Local authorities are not simply importers of private sector goods or services, they also exercise key controls over certain private sector activities, for example through their licensing functions and through granting or withholding planning permission in land use and development. Both these functions provide opportunities for corrupt activities to bring about a lucrative outcome for a private entrepreneur, that may not be certain by legitimate means.

Particularly vulnerable authorities are those which have a history of unchallenged one-party dominance, where there is no effective opposition and where investigations or complaints are likely to be frustrated by the local 'party machine'. The Salmon Commission recognised that local authority policy decisions are often taken by an inner caucus of the majority party, not subject to local government law or standing orders, and merely rubber stamped by a party-controlled council. They overlooked, however, a further obstacle to critical opposition and openness in local government – the existence of 'town hall lodges' and the way in which Freemason activities can become mechanisms of informal organisation. Although the Freemason movement is officially opposed to discussion of politics in the course of its meetings,[11] it does not necessarily follow that in practice the order is of no political significance. The Society of Labour Lawyers in evidence to the Salmon Commission alleged that town hall lodges existed at all of the local authorities concerned in the criminal proceedings arising from the Poulson affair, and involved almost all of the defendants. Membership was said to include leading councillors *across the political divide*, past councillors who held positions with firms contracting with the council, and a limited number of senior officers, all to the prejudice of public discussion and decision-making.[12]

In reviewing the network of legal, administrative and discretionary rules designed to safeguard against the pressures and incentives for conflict of interest and corruption in local government, we must be aware of the distinction traditionally drawn between two types of public servant: the elected local councillor and the appointed local government employee. Councillors serve for a specified term of office and are ultimately responsible to the local electorate. They are not full-time salaried politicians, but they are entitled to claim an attendance allowance for approved duties. Local government officers are permanently appointed and are responsible to their employing authority. They have different but complementary roles, with the appointed officer providing councillors with advice and information and directed to carry out the council's work. These functional differences in part account for significant variations in the legal and procedural requirements of conflict of interest provisions applying to members and officers.

Legal safeguards

As we saw in chapter 2, the major legal penalties for bribery and corruption in local government reside in the three Acts known collectively as the Prevention of Corruption Acts. A check on financial probity is also one of the functions of the external audit which is a statutory requirement for all local authorities and is in addition to the internal audit. In England and Wales the majority of local authorities are audited by district auditors, a few by approved private auditors; both work under a strict code of practice laid down by central government. In Scotland the external audit procedure is centrally organised by a Commission for Local Authority Accounts.

Legislation has also been used in a preventive role to safeguard against conflict between private interests and public office. Prior to the Local Government Act, 1933 it was the general rule that persons who had a share or interest in any contract or employment with a council were barred from membership of that council. The Royal Commission on Local Government that reported in 1929 took stock of the practical problems arising from this ruling and recommended that the nineteenth-century legislation should be revised. Its proposal that the disqualification should apply to voting rather than membership of a council was enacted in the Local Government Act, 1933. The provisions were affirmed in the Local Government Act, 1972 and the Local Government (Scotland) Act, 1973.

Neither the Redcliffe-Maud Committee nor the Salmon Commission found evidence of a desire to return to a situation whereby private interests disqualified individuals from becoming councillors. However, the Redcliffe-Maud Committee observed:

> There is one area where the connection between a councillor's private interests and his activities in the authority appears to be so close as to give colour, however unjustifiably, to suggestions of a corrupt or improper motive. This is membership of a particular committee by a councillor whose personal or private activities are closely related to its subject. (para 68)

Of particular concern were councillors involved with planning and development control and who had private professional interests in land transactions. Although aware of the sensitivity of this issue, the Redcliffe-Maud Committee concluded that given the scope of responsibility of local government, legal prohibitions on service on 'interest-related committees' would be difficult to define and operate satisfactorily. They also felt that such prohibitions were undesirable because in their opinion, individuals with private interests and occupations make a 'valuable' contribution to local government; a view endorsed by the Salmon Commission.

Thus, private interests are currently not a bar to membership of a local authority, but once elected a local councillor is expected to comply with strict disclosure requirements when engaging in official business. These requirements were originally contained in the Local Government Act, 1933 (Sections 76 ff.). They are now restated in the Local Government Act, 1972 (Sections 94–98, 105 and 117) and the Local Government (Scotland) Act, 1973 (Sections 38–42, 60 and 68).

These Acts lay down that a councillor who has a direct or indirect pecuniary interest in any contract proposed or any other matter before the authority must at any meeting disclose this interest as soon as practicable, except in situations where he has given a general written notice. Subsequent to disclosing his interest, he must not speak or vote on the matter. Failure to comply with these provisions carries a penalty of a fine not exceeding £200 for each offence, unless the defendant can prove he did not know that the matter in which he had a pecuniary interest was under consideration at the meeting.

If it wishes, the local authority may take stronger measures by providing in its standing orders for the exclusion of a councillor from any meeting of the authority when a matter in which he has a direct or indirect pecuniary interest is under discussion. In all instances a member's interest includes those of his spouse if known. An indirect interest arises where a member is associated as director, shareholder, partner or employee, with a body or person who has a direct interest in the matter under discussion. In practice, a member may apply directly to the appropriate Secretary of State, or ask the local authority to apply on his behalf, for a dispension to speak and/or vote on the matter in which he has an interest.

As an alternative to the procedure of oral disclosure in the meeting, where an interest arises because a member or his spouse is a member, partner or employee of a body which is transacting with the authority, or is the tenant of premises owned by the authority, he may give a general written notice of his interest. In conjunction with these legal requirements, local authorities are required to maintain a statutory register of notices and oral disclosures. These are open to inspection by members of the council and, if the authority's standing orders permit, to any local government elector.

The disclosure requirements under the Local Government Acts are different for local government officers. Officers are only required to disclose pecuniary interests in contracts before the council. They do not have to make an oral disclosure at meetings but they do have to give written notice of any interest, direct or indirect, in any contract the authority engages in or intends to enter. An officer is also precluded from accepting a fee or reward, other than his official salary, for actions undertaken in his official capacity. Breach of either of these provisions is a criminal offence and carries a maximum fine of £200.

Register of interests

Both the Redcliffe-Maud Committee and the Salmon Commission recommended a statutory register of pecuniary interests for councillors, to be used as a supplement and not as an alternative to oral disclosure. Neither body was so naive as to imagine that such a procedure by itself would prevent unethical conduct. This was not its main purpose. As the Redcliffe-Maud Committee explained:

> A register . . . might indeed be to a large extent an exercise in public relations, but we regard that as a justification rather than a criticism of it, since public opinion about local government is at the heart of the problem with which we are concerned. (para 58)

A register would serve two purposes: firstly, to act as a guideline to the conduct of an 'interested member' and to provide a background against which his actions could be challenged; secondly, to function as a symbolic demonstration of openness.

Recognising that the acceptance of such a register would depend on a reasonable balance between the need for openness and the councillor's individual right to privacy, the Redcliffe-Maud Committee recommended that the content should simply denote their existence without going into detail of the amount involved, and should include interests of the councillor's spouse but no other relative. Bearing this in mind, the format of interests recommended for registration can be summarised as follows:

(1) All paid employments and occupations, including directorships, consultancies, and any sponsorship of the member by any organisation or person . . . .
(2) All land or other real property in the area of the authority, owned freehold, or held on a lease granted for one year or more, or in respect of which an option to purchase is held . . . .
(3) Companies or other bodies where the member has a beneficial interest in securities of a nominal value greater than £1,000 or one-hundredth of the issued share capital, whichever is the less . . . Investment trusts and unit trusts should be excluded.
(4) Any tenancy of premises owned by the authority.
(para 60)

The Redcliffe-Maud Committee also recommended a statutory register of interests for senior council officers and certain other officers designated by the authority; for example in the planning or estates departments, who exercise particularly sensitive responsibilities. Drawing on the distinction between the councillor who is responsible to the electorate and the officer who is responsible to the authority, the Committee suggested that the officers' register should be open to inspection by councillors only, not by electors as should be the case with the councillors' register. Also calling in defence this distinction between the two types of public servant, the Salmon Commission found they could not support the case for a statutory register of interests for officers.

So far Parliament has not found the inclination to introduce legislation for a statutory register of interests for either group. It is therefore discretionary as to whether a local authority incorporates into its standing orders a register of interests for councillor and/or officers, and responsive authorities are not obliged to adopt the model recommended by the Redcliffe-Maud Committee. This creates a diversity of practice among local authorities and raises a number of questions regarding the extent to which registers have been adopted, the nature of their content and the procedures for their maintenance and inspection. It is hoped that the research into standards of conduct in local government currently being undertaken at Teesside Polytechnic will provide us with some insight into these and related questions.[13]

A code of conduct

Non-pecuniary interests are not specifically covered by the legal disclosure requirements but the Redcliffe-Maud Committee encouraged members to treat them in the same spirit as pecuniary interests. They also envisaged members would obtain some guidance through another of their major recommendations – a national code of conduct. This would have two purposes: firstly to provide authoritative guidance on ethical conduct to councillors; secondly to set down a clear public standard by which conduct in local government could be measured by those outside it.

Prior to 1974 a written code of conduct did not exist, although the Committee recognised that to a large extent the principles embodied in their draft Code were those already governing the 'best practices' among councillors. Summing up the content of the Code, which was supplementary to law and standing orders, the Committee recommended:

> In addition to drawing attention to the law and standing orders, the code should deal with such matters as the distinction between public and private interest, membership of interest-related committees, the relationships between members and employees, the use of official facilities, and the handling of confidential information. (para 171)

The Code was intended primarily for councillors, but its spirit had relevance for officers.

In October 1975 an amended version of the draft Code was annexed to a joint circular from the Department of the Environment, the Scottish Development Department and the Welsh Office (DOE circular 94/75, SDD circular 97/75 and WO circular 166/75) to all local authorities in England, Wales and Scotland. This urged authorities 'to bring the Code to the attention of all members of councils and committees and to give it wide publicity'. A majority of local authorities have responded by incorporating the Code into their standing orders.

Although the Code was urged upon local authorities by central government, it was not embodied in legislation. Therefore it would seem reasonable to assume that its status is advisory. However, the Commissioners for Local Administration[14] appear to work with a different interpretation. As failure by a councillor to disclose a non-pecuniary interest in a matter is not covered by statutory provisions, it may come within the jurisdiction of the Commission for Local Administration as a ground for maladministration by the authority. In their annual report in 1981 the Commissioners for England judged:

> . . . the failure of a member to act in accordance with the standards set by the National Code can be maladministration even though the Code, or a variation on it, has not been adopted by his authority.[15]

Here the Code is elevated from a discretionary document in an advisory capacity to an authoritative statement of principles against which a member's conduct can be measured, regardless of whether his own authority has adopted the Code or not. The Commission cannot investigate or penalise an individual member as is the case with the legal requirement to disclose pecuniary interests, but the Commission can find the authority guilty of maladministration.

Outside employment

The civil service and the armed forces are the only groups in the public sector currently bound by rules about employment on retirement or resignation. The Redcliffe-Maud Committee felt that similar dangers faced local government employees entering private practice as faced civil servants. The prospect of a job in the private sector could colour their actions while they were still employed by the authority. Also by taking their knowledge of local government procedures into private practice as, for example, solicitors or planning consultants, they could give their clients an improper edge over competitors. In consequence, they recommended that the national scheme of conditions of service for local government officers should incorporate a rule which would prohibit senior or professional employees entering private employment in an authority's area without the authority's permission within two years of resignation or retirement. The Salmon Commission disagreed with this recommendation but aware of the potential for criticism surrounding movement to the private sector, encouraged local authorities to 'appraise their own needs in this field' (para 209).

Diversity of Practice

Although they share a similar long-term goal of maintaining a high standard of probity in public life, different sectors of the public service have developed their own style and procedures for ensuring ethical conduct. Thus, evaluation of the charge that the House of Commons has been less vigilant in putting its own House in order than it has been in recommending the standards for other public servants to keep is far from straightforward.

As it stands, the charge places too much weight on the interest and interference of the House of Commons in the problems and domestic arrangements of other sectors of the public service. Both the civil service and local government operate a complex network of rules and conventions for ensuring ethical conduct, only a limited part of which derives directly from Parliament in the form of legal requirements. True, Parliament has seen fit to set up two official inquiries into standards of conduct in central and local government, but to a large extent this has had the effect of 'passing the buck' to outside bodies. A case in point is the issue of a register of interests. Asked by a backbencher in 1975 whether he would 'bring forward legislation to establish a compulsory register of interests for all peers, councillors, senior civil servants, senior council officials and others in the upper reaches of public life', the Home Secretary replied, 'no, a proposal of this kind would come within the remit of the Royal Commission on Standards of Conduct in Public Life' (*HC Debs* 897:1975, 424). In 1976 the Salmon Commission went ahead and recommended a register of pecuniary interests for councillors but eight years have passed and the House of Commons, although adopting registration for itself, has shown no inclination to legally impose the same on local councillors.

It is also extremely difficult to make generalisations about the stringency of rules in other institutions engaged in the public service. The most fundamental observation about procedures regulating standards of conduct in local government is their diversity and unevenness of practice. All local authorities are subject to the legal provisions contained in the Local Government Acts for the disclosure of pecuniary interests, and to external surveillance in terms of external audit. For the most part their standing orders will also contain the draft code of conduct or a variant upon it. However, the other recommendations emerging from the Redcliffe-Maud Committee or the Salmon Commission are discretionary, and it is up to each individual authority to decide to what extent, if at all, to take them on board. And even when they are responsive to model provisions, each authority is likely to implement them in its own style. Even in the civil service where more centralisation is to be expected, there is an emphasis, where possible, on delegation to individual departments both in the making of rules of conduct and in disciplinary matters.

Nevertheless, in this and earlier chapters we have established that there are significant differences between the rules of conduct governing MPs and those found in other sectors of public life. The most fundamental difference is one of *principle*; that is the claim by the House to be the sole judge of Members and procedures, immune from outside investigations. We debated this claim to exclusive self-discipline in the previous chapter, and saw that one outcome which sets MPs apart from other public servants is that MPs in their parliamentary capacity are not thought to be subject to the Prevention of Corruption Acts. Another difference in legal requirements exists between MPs and councillors. Whereas an MP is simply required by resolution of the House to declare any relevant pecuniary interests or benefits in any debate or proceeding of the House, a local councillor is not only legally obliged to disclose at any meeting any direct or indirect pecuniary interest in the matter under debate, he must also refrain from speaking or voting on the matter. We have also seen that in contrast to the written guidance for ministers, or the strict procedural guidelines for civil servants, local government councillors and local government employees, there is no comparable rule book for MPs.

Functional Differences

Successive Governments have argued that functional differences between the House and other sectors of the public service account for these differences of stringency in the rules regulating ethical conduct. For example, when asked by a backbencher in 1968 whether he would agree that there was a discrepancy between the rules governing pecuniary interests in Parliament, and the seemingly more stringent rules in local government, the Prime Minister (Harold Wilson) explained:

> There is this difference. This House is a legislature, whereas the members of a local authority are an executive as well as, in certain cases, a legislature. That is the difference. (*HC Debs* 767:1968, 1689)

In 1973 Richard Crossman gave a more colourful description of the functional difference between Ministers and MPs:

> Of the 625 Members of the House of Commons it is only the ministers who take part in decisions and carry departmental responsibilities which render them open to corruption. As ministers they are required to obey an elaborate written code of behaviour. Up to now the backbench MP has been exempt largely because he runs nothing, decides nothing, and usually knows nothing worth paying for.[16]

The main defence of existing arrangements therefore has been that you cannot apply the same arguments to MPs as you can, for example, to local councillors, Ministers or civil servants, because MPs are not 'doing' anything in terms of executive action. Therefore they are less exposed to situations of conflict of interest with the risk of corruption. Moreover, as we saw in chapter 4, constitutional limits are set to Members' powers to confer direct financial benefit on their constituents or other individuals or groups. Added to this there is the defence of the representative dimension of the elected Member of Parliament. That democratic government implies an MP is properly subject to a whole range of outside interests and influences which may induce him to ask parliamentary questions, speak or vote a certain way in the House, table amendments to legislation, contact ministers and so on. Stricter rules for MPs could be rejected on the grounds they might be impractical or they might infringe the legitimate representative function of Members. Then there is also the contrast between the 'career' or the appointed official and the uncertain tenure of the elected Member to be taken into account.

It becomes obvious that there *are* functional and occupational differences between MPs and other public servants, although these are rarely as clear cut as successive Governments would like to think. The issue is whether these differences justify varying degrees of stringency in the rules and guidelines prescribing and circumscribing proper conduct. This inevitably begs the question as to how much influence an MP actually has. To gain some insight into these issues I asked the thirty MPs included in my sample survey what aspects of being an MP in their view provided opportunities for conflict of interest and possible corrupt activity. To avoid difficulties and ambiguities which might present themselves to Members who had already said that conflict of interest in a non-pecuniary sense was inevitable and endemic to politics, Members were asked to restrict their understanding of conflict of interest to direct or indirect financial interests.

In attempting to justify why registration should be restricted to MPs and no other groups one Labour MP said,

> I think MPs are in a special category because they have power to influence events . . . this power can be used by outside interests by bribery and corruption to influence the course of events.

This was not a view shared by other Members in the sample who stressed the limitations on the scope and extent of the influence wielded by individual MPs. The general consensus confirmed the popular image that backbenchers do not have much power in decision-making. However this did not prevent MPs from recognising potential opportunities for advancing outside interests and the importance of justice being *seen* to be done.

Two main aspects of the MP's role were cited by Members as providing the potential opportunities for advancing outside interests: firstly, an MP's behaviour on the floor of the House or in committee; and secondly, the unique qualification of having access to Ministers and civil servants. Whether or not it is exploited, there is scope for a Member to promote outside interests on the floor of the House or in committees. For example, a Member who is a company director or consultant could conceivably promote the company's interests through parliamentary questions, speaking or voting in the House, tabling amendments to legislation, or even initiating legislation in the form of Private Members' Bills.

Select committee membership raises the particularly delicate problem of balancing knowledge of the subject under discussion with impartial judgment. A recent illustration of this dilemma was provided by the Committee stage of the Cable and Broadcasting Bill, where proceedings were dominated by MPs who could be seen to have a potential interest in the outcome of the Bill. It was reported (*Observer*, 1.7.1984) that at least half of the backbench Conservative MPs declared either a direct or indirect financial interest during the course of the Committee's proceedings, and some of the Labour Committee members also had interests in the form of union sponsorships. The benefit, so it is often argued, lies in having well-informed legislators who openly declare their interests and can enlighten their less knowledgeable colleagues. The cost lies in the scope for real or apparent conflict between public and private interest. On this occasion the unusually high concentration of experts, well briefed by skilled parliamentary lobbyists, drew criticism, even from some senior Conservative MPs. It has to be recognised that while it is useful to include among the membership of a select committee some MPs with a knowledge of the matter under discussion, where this knowledge derives from an outside financial interest or employment a conflict of interest could arise which the individual MP would then have to resolve; possibly by resigning from membership of the committee.

A Member can also advance outside interests through his facility of access to people of influence, namely Ministers and civil servants. A Member can write to or have direct contact with a Minister about a business matter without necessarily declaring an interest and persuade him to take action. He can also elicit information which may be extremely valuable to a particular firm or industry seeking advance knowledge of the way in which politics are moving in their field.

In addition to these two major sources or points of influence, an MP can also act as a focus of opinion in the House for a particular outside interest, hiring rooms where a meeting, exhibition or press conference may take place and ensuring that other MPs are aware of the event.

Thus, even if in practice the amount of influence wielded by individual MPs is low, this does not eliminate the problem of conflict of interest. Recent anxiety has highlighted not only the problem of actual conflict, but also the *appearance* of conflict. This might be created by the mere existence of these opportunities, even though they may not necessarily be exploited. As Joe Ashton (Lab) explained to me when discussing the problems of public relations activity, even if MPs themselves know they have little influence, outsiders may not. The image of the influential MP may be a myth, but it is still important if it is believed and shapes people's behaviour. Furthermore, a public relations firm may employ an MP for no other skill or purpose than the fact that he is an MP and has prestige value, regardless of any influence he may or may not in fact possess.

On these grounds there is a strong argument for the House of Commons being seen to take a tougher line on standards of conduct. A review of MPs' status under the Prevention of Corruption Acts was suggested in the previous chapter. Another useful step would be a consolidation of the *ad hoc* rules and conventions of parliamentary etiquette into a coherent code of moral instructions, brought to the attention of sitting Members and to each and every newly elected MP. A controversial but logical sequel to this would be to review the possible sanctions for breaches of such a code.

Public Trust

Finally, a separate argument in support of different sets of rules regulating pecuniary interests for different sectors of the public service has been constructed on the basis of public trust. This was evident, for example, in a Green Paper on Members of Parliament and Conflict of Interest issued by the Canadian Parliament in 1973. Having discussed the difference between the principles of disclosure and avoidance with regard to pecuniary interest, this report recommended against making a strict choice between these two schools of thought on the grounds that, 'neither position is totally and absolutely indefensible and that the nature of public trust ought to be a major factor in determining the application of any one of these philosophies'.[17] From this position they concluded that rules on conflict of interest which apply to Cabinet Ministers need not necessarily be imposed on MPs and other public officials. As we have discovered in earlier chapters it would seem that a high level of public trust has been vested in Members of Parliament in the past and can be traced back in representation theory to the nineteenth-century conception of the MP as a trustee. Generally speaking, Members of Parliament have simply been trusted to comply with the moral dictum of placing the public interest before their own advantage. The public and parliamentary anxiety which provoked the establishment of the Register of Interests in the House of Commons may, however, signal declining confidence in this arrangement. As Lord Houghton has argued, the issue at stake is not simply the narrow one of Members' financial interests. The larger issue of the credibility of politicians, political parties and their leaders is being questioned.[18]

8 The Experience of the American Congress

In contrast to the British House of Commons which relies on parliamentary tradition and a minimum of written rules, the American Congress has in recent years opted for a more codified approach to safeguarding against conflict of interest among its members. The current measures are largely a product of the stringent ethics codes introduced by both chambers of Congress in 1977, and in the 1978 Ethics in Government Act. In order to appreciate the significance of these provisions, it is useful first to take a brief look at the measures which preceded them and the wider constitutional framework in which they operate. Key factors in this framework are the salaries and allowances available to Representatives and Senators.

Salaries and Allowances

In December 1982 Representatives voted themselves a 15 per cent ($9,100) pay rise. This lifted their annual salary to $69,800 and, breaking with nearly two centuries of tradition, marked the first time that Representatives were to be paid more than Senators. Since the first Congress in 1789 members of both chambers had been paid the same salary except for one year (1795–6) when Senators were paid $7 a day and Representatives $6. The permanent conversion from a per diem compensation to an annual congressional salary was finally achieved in August 1856, when the then daily rate of $8 was exchanged for an annual salary of $3,000.

In July 1983 Senators restored parity with the House by raising their salaries to $69,800. In January 1984, under the social security rescue plan approved by Congress in the previous March, Congressmen started paying social security taxes for the first time. However, this annual deduction from their salary of around $2,500 was offset by the automatic cost of living pay rise. Effective from 1 January 1984, this 3.5 per cent rise increased their salaries by almost $2,500 to $72,243.

A 1981 law (*PL* 97–51) provides an automatic appropriation of money for this rise without the need to take a politically sensitive vote. However, the salary increase could be rescinded if Congressmen thought public criticism warranted it, and in January 1984 the Senate approved a bill (*S*–2211) revoking the increase for both Chambers. This has to be approved by the House for the salary decrease to take effect, and the House is reported to have no plans to bring the measure approved by the Senate to the floor. *Congressional Quarterly Weekly Report* (11.2.1984) speculates that electoral pressure to cut congressional salaries would probably cause the bill to be approved if it did reach the floor of the House.

In addition to their congressional salaries Members have given themselves a plethora of expense allowances to cover expenditure incurred in running congressional offices both in Washington and in their home districts. The two most substantial perquisites are the personal staff allowance and the 'official expenses' allowances.[1]

In 1982 the value of the personal staff allowance for each Representative was $352,536 per year. Within this allowance Members could hire up to 18 full-time and four temporary aides in their Washington and district offices. For Senators, the value of the personal staff allowance varies with the size of the state represented. In 1982 the allowance ranged from $621,054 per year for states with a population of less than 2 million to $1,247,879 for states with more than 21 million residents. Senators can employ as many aides as they wish within the value of the allowance. This averages between 25 and 60 aides.

The 'official expense' allowance is separate from the personal staff allowance and covers domestic travel, stationery, newsletters, postage, telephone and telegraph service and office expenses in Washington and in the Member's congressional district or state. The total amount of the expense allowance available to Representatives varies, depending on factors such as the location of a Member's district and its proximity to Washington. In 1982 the average House allowance was estimated to be $103,000. The size of Senators' official expense allowance also varies, depending on the population size of the state represented and its distance from Washington. In 1982 the annual expense allowance for Senators ranged from $33,000 for a Senator from Delaware to $143,000 for a Senator from Hawaii, averaging out at around $55,000.

In addition to these perquisites of office, Members have traditionally supplemented their congressional salaries with earned and unearned outside income from various financial, business and professional activities. A particularly profitable source of earned income is by way of honoraria – delivering speeches, making public appearances, broadcasts and publishing articles for fees or royalties. The problems associated with this practice and with other forms of outside interests and employment will become clear in the ensuing discussion of ethical conduct in Congress.

Past Concern with Ethical Conduct

Concern for the ethical conduct of Members of Congress can be found in the Constitution, in Senate and House Rules and in Federal Statutes. The activities of Congressmen are limited by several sections of the United States Code. The series of laws in Title 18 of the Code make it a federal crime for Congressmen to accept a bribe or otherwise abuse their office for financial gain. Congress has also used statute law to regulate campaign contributions and expenditures, to limit the amount Members can earn in honoraria and to prohibit nepotism by federal officials including Senators and Representatives. It has also used legislation (Federal Regulation of Lobbying Act, 1946) in an attempt to check the mass of lobbies and pressure groups which seek to recruit the services of Congressmen.

However, the fundamental approach of Congress in handling conflict of interest among its members derives from the constitutional provision that

> Each House may determine the Rules of its Proceedings, punish its Members for disorderly Behaviour, and, with the concurrence of two-thirds, expel a Member. (Article 1, Section 5, Clause 2)

Yet prior to the adoption of a specific code of ethics in 1968 Congress displayed little enthusiasm for establishing precise and binding rules of good behaviour for itself. The main protection against unethical behaviour lay in the vigilance of a critical press and the periodic requirement of re-election.

The main safeguard written into House Rules concerned voting. Deriving from Jefferson's 1801 rule, each Representative is required to vote 'unless he has a direct personal or pecuniary interest in the event of such a question'. He may vote for his private interests if the measure is not for his exclusive benefit but for that of a group. In contrast, Senate Rules require that each Senator must vote on a question unless specifically excused by the Senate, even if by doing so he experiences a conflict of interest.

In 1946 the Senate rejected a resolution introduced by Senator Wayne Morse which would have required Senators to file with the Secretary of the Senate an annual statement on sources of income and transactions in securities and commodities. Senator Morse had introduced this resolution at a time of growing concern over the lack of clear ethical standards for the conduct of government employees and officers. He was also responding to public criticism of the practice of Members accepting money from speeches and other outside activities to supplement their congressional salaries. While the acceptance of honoraria payments was above board, many of the organisations or groups making the payments were seen to have obvious legislative interests and were suspected of using honoraria payments as a lobbying tactic.

A staunch defender of the propriety of outside interests and activities, Morse nevertheless believed that the electorate was entitled to know about the sources of income of their Members. Introducing his measure to the Senate he had explained:

> My resolution is bottomed upon the very sound philosophical principle enunciated by Plutarch that Caesar's wife must be above suspicion. Likewise, I feel that, so far as the public's evaluation of Members of the Senate is concerned, they must be above suspicion . . . my resolution . . . is in keeping with the public's right to know what influences may possibly be brought to bear on Members of the Senate in the performance of their legislative duties. (*Congressional Record*, v.92, 23 July 1946, p. 9741)

Although subsequent attempts by Senator Morse to introduce financial disclosure legislation were also defeated, he gathered support for his cause among other Members of Congress. Furthermore, in a special message to Congress in September 1951 President Harry Truman advocated legislation requiring annual public financial disclosure statements by officers and designated employees of Congress, the Executive and the Judiciary.

From this time until the appointment of the Senate Select Committee on Standards and Conduct in 1964, there were several unsuccessful attempts to persuade Congress to set up joint or select committees to review ethical standards and to command stricter guidelines for official conduct. There were also minor developments in the general precepts urged upon Members in the performance of their congressional duties. In 1958 Congress approved a ten-point, general code of ethical conduct for all government employees, including Congressmen. Introduced by Representative Charles Bennett, this was intended primarily as a guide for the individual's conscience. Adopted as a concurrent resolution (H.Con. Res. 175) the provisions have no legally binding effect, but the standards contained therein are still expected to be observed by Members 'ever conscious that public office is a public trust'. They are frequently cited by the Ethics Committees in disciplinary cases.

During the mid-1960s several well-publicised allegations of improper conduct involving Congressmen forced a reluctant Congress to take a closer look at the official conduct of its Members and employees. In particular, the resignation of Senator Robert G. (Bobby) Baker in 1963 from his post as Secretary to the Senate Democratic Majority threw into sharp relief the disquieting situation whereby serious allegations could be levelled against Senators or Senate employees, and the Senate for its part could provide no specific ethical guidelines for official conduct.

The Senate Rules and Administration Committee was directed to look into the allegations surrounding the Baker affair. More generally it investigated the financial and business interests and activities of Senators and Senate employees. The Committee found that many of Baker's outside interests and activities had been in conflict with his official duties and responsibilities. They made several recommendations, including the proposal that the Senate should adopt rules on public financial disclosure.

In a subsequent report the Rules Committee clarified the general sentiment in the Senate concerning the outside interests and activities of Members. It was keen to point out that during its hearings it had found no evidence of a desire to restrict the outside interests and employment of Members, simply an impression that disclosure of outside pecuniary interests was now considered advisable.

The Committee's recommendations for additional Senate Rules on ethical conduct were embodied in S. Res. 377. This subsequently languished with the eighty-eighth Congress. In the meantime, Senator John Sherman Cooper, a member of the Rules Committee, gained Senate approval for his proposal for a permanent Select Committee of the Senate to inquire into allegations of misconduct, advise on disciplinary action if necessary and to keep under review the efficacy of Senate rules on ethical conduct. A request by the Rules Committee for jurisdiction to perform these functions had previously been turned down.

Accordingly a permanent Select Committee on Standards and Conduct was appointed by the Senate in 1964 to investigate cases of misconduct and to formulate an ethical code. This six-member bipartisan Committee marked the first time an internal disciplinary body had been set up in either Chamber of Congress on a continuing basis. Two years later the House was confronted with speculation and rumour concerning the conduct of Representative Adam Clayton Powell Jr. (Democrat, New York). Powell was alleged to have misused congressional funds, his chief indiscretion being nepotism – the hiring of his wife as a paid member of his congressional staff when she in fact did not work either in his home district or in his Washington office. Largely as a response to this affair, the House followed the lead of the Senate and established a Standing Committee on Standards of Official Conduct. This had the sole function of recommending a code of conduct.

As a result, both Chambers adopted specific rules of conduct for the first time in 1968. The new ethics provisions in the Senate set out in S. Res. 266 covered four areas: outside employment, campaign contributions, political fund raising, and financial disclosure. The latter rule required annual financial disclosure statements to be filed with the Comptroller General of the United States. With the exception of gifts in excess of $50 and honoraria of $300 or more these statements were to remain confidential. No new provisions were introduced for punishing wilful violation of these rules.

The House ethics provisions were contained in H. Res. 1099 which laid down an eight-point Code of Official Conduct for Members, officers and employees and a new disclosure rule. The latter was broader than that for Senators and required annual disclosure of interests in any firm doing 'substantial' business with the Federal Government or subject to federal regulatory agencies in which ownership exceeded $5,000 or income $1,000, professional practice from which they received $1,000 or more and the source of income for services when this exceeded $5,000 annually. The dollar value for assets or sources of income thus disclosed had to be filed but remained confidential.

The 1968 ethics provisions marked the first time in 180 years of congressional history that members were obliged to make a limited public financial disclosure. At this time, however, neither Chamber thought it necessary or desirable to place any restrictions on Members' earnings over and above their official salary. The emphasis was clearly on disclosure.

Renewed Allegations Lead to Reforms

Despite these specific measures, during the early 1970s numerous charges of unethical or illegal conduct in Congress were made and in 1976 both Chambers were prompted to take further action to put their own houses in order. Numbered among these charges were the cases of Representative Robert L.F. Sikes (Democrat, Florida) charged with failure to disclose certain banking and industrial stock according to House Rules, and Representative Wayne L. Hays (Democrat, Ohio) charged with keeping a mistress on the House payroll. Sikes was reprimanded by the House in July 1976 and Hays was forced to resign his Chairmanship of the House Administration Committee. He later resigned from Congress. There were also pervasive allegations that some Members had accepted illegal campaign contributions from Gulf Oil, and in another instance in 1976 eighteen members of Congress – including both Chairmen of the House and Senate Ethics Committees – admitted receiving unreported free hunting trips from various defence contracts. All these events were taking place against the background of the Watergate affair which had prompted both Houses of Congress to lead inquiries into the Executive, and which had created a climate of public concern about morality in government.

Moreover, a Federal Salary Commission urged in its December 1976 Report that the pay rise for top officials in the legislative, judicial and executive branches, which was due to take effect on 20 February 1977, should be tied to the adoption of a stricter code of conduct. The Commission argued:

> Such a reform must be sufficiently tangible to persuade a substantial majority of Americans that the post-Watergate era has truly begun . . . Such a majority is by no means persuaded now.[2]

A cap on outside income

In July 1976 the House appointed a bi-partisan fifteen-member Commission on Administrative Review which, under the chairmanship of Representative David Obey (Democrat, Wisconsin), was directed to study and make recommendations on improving the administrative procedures of the House. In December the Speaker directed this Commission to make recommendations concerning ethical practices and financial accountability. On 18 January 1977, six months after the House's initiative, the Senate agreed by voice vote to set up a fifteen-member Committee, chaired by Senator Gaylord Nelson (Democrat, Wisconsin) to formulate a code of ethics. In both Chambers the task of drawing up a new ethics code was entrusted to a special committee or commission and not given to the existing Ethics Committees. These were coming under criticism for their lack of disciplinary action over charges of congressional misconduct.

On 14 February 1977 the Obey Commission reported its recommendations to amend the Rules of the House with respect to the Code of Official Conduct and financial disclosure among other matters. After vigorous and often partisan discussion in three separate standing committees these proposals were adopted almost intact by the House by a vote of 402–22 (H. Res. 287). The most significant and controversial change introduced was the outside earned income limitation rule. Hailed by Speaker O'Neill as 'the heart and soul of the entire package', this prohibited any member from earning income at a job outside Congress in excess of 15 per cent of his official salary, effective from 31 December 1978.

This income cap marked a fundamental change in Congress's tactics in combating conflict of interest. Prior to this both Chambers had relied almost exclusively on disclosure to curb the problem and had not thought it necessary or desirable to restrict or prohibit members' outside interests and employment. Commenting retrospectively the House Select Committee on Ethics said:

> Two major considerations prompted the adoption of the rule. First, substantial payments to a Member of Congress for rendering 'personal services' to outside groups presents a significant and avoidable potential for conflict of interest. Second, it is inconsistent with the concept that being a Member of Congress is a full-time job to permit a Member to have substantial earnings from other employment.[3]

Opponents of the rule criticised it primarily on two grounds: either because it did not touch unearned income such as dividends from stocks or bonds; or precisely because they feared it would create a class of professional full-time politicians. The tradition of members earning income from public speeches or articles was likewise disrupted with the introduction of a prohibition on members from accepting any individual honorarium of more than $750.

H. Res. 287 also introduced considerably tighter public financial disclosure provisions than before, thereby forcing members to give up some of their privacy in financial dealings. Members were required to file an annual disclosure statement with the Clerk of the House showing the source and amount of all income received from a single source aggregating $100 or more and the source and value of gifts from a single source aggregating $100 or more per year. This disclosure statement also covered certain reimbursements, financial holdings, liabilities, securities, commodity transactions and real estate. Moreover, declaration of the financial dealings of the spouse of the person reporting was required if these were 'under constructive control of the person reporting'. Whereas under the 1968 code the precise amounts of holdings remained confidential, under H. Res. 287 the financial disclosure reports were ordered to be printed and made public by the Clerk of the House.

The code had several other provisions; for example, the ending of unofficial office accounts by which means Members had accepted unreported contributions from organisations and individuals and used the money for virtually any purpose they chose; new restrictions on the use of the Member's frank; and new restrictions and prohibitions on foreign travel.

Senate rules tightened

The Nelson Committee reported its recommendations for a new Senate ethics code on 24 February 1977 (S. Res. 110). As so many of the provisions were declared unenforceable by members of the Senate Ethics Committee (formerly called the Senate Select Committee on Standards of Conduct) who would be charged with enforcing the code, S. Res. 110 was overhauled even before it reached the floor. However, the new version retained the basic scope of the code and on 1 April 1977, after two weeks of debate and action on 64 amendments, it was agreed by the Senate. The vote of 86–9 belied the strength of feeling against the code among Senators who had voted for the resolution largely because when the Senate had accepted the $12,900 pay rise in February, both the Democratic Majority Leader, Robert C. Byrd, and the Republican Minority Leader, Howard H. Baker Jr., had pledged they would support a limit on outside earned income.

The broad outlines of the Senate code were similar to that adopted by the House with the addition of some extra provisions, including the enforcement of the code by the Senate Committee on Ethics. The most controversial change was the limit on outside earned income to 15 per cent of a Senator's official salary, to take effect on 30 September 1979. Within two months of this rule being adopted, five Senators headed by Republican Senator Paul Laxalt, were challenging in Federal Court the constitutionality of the Senate's action in imposing an outside earned income limit on its members.[4]

S. Res. 110 also limited to $1,000 the amount a Senator could receive as an honorarium for making a speech, appearance or writing an article. Under the new financial disclosure requirements all Senators and Senate employees making $25,000 or more a year were required to file with the Secretary of the Senate a statement of their financial interests – assets, holdings, liabilities and transactions – and the source of all income of their spouses and dependants. The disclosure provisions extended to candidates for the Senate, although they could not be binding on anyone outside the Senate. Senators, their spouses and their dependants were also prohibited from accepting gifts of over $100 in aggregate value during a year from anyone having a direct interest in legislation before Congress or from any foreign national acting on behalf of a foreign organisation, business or government. Although a specific section of the Senate code was devoted to a series of conflict of interest provisions (Rule 45, now known as Rule 37), the Nelson Committee who formulated the code stressed that, '. . . concern about conflict of interest underlies most, if not all, of the Rules making up the Code of Conduct'.[5]

1978 Ethics in Government Act

The ethics codes as written into House and Senate Rules were enforceable only by internal penalties such as reprimand, censure, expulsion or loss of seniority. However, the Ethics in Government Act, 1978 (S555 –PL 95–521) codified the public financial disclosure provisions of both Chambers and enabled civil penalties, in particular fines, to be imposed for wilful violations. This Act was passed in the wake of the Watergate scandal and at a time when President Carter had made ethics an important issue. There had also been considerable government activity at State level with respect to financial disclosure legislation. As of August 1977 about 36 States required some form of annual financial disclosure by public officials.

Title 1 of the Ethics in Government Act required disclosure of earned income by source, type and amount, unearned income by categories of value (e.g. $5,000–$15,000 and $15,000–$50,000) and honoraria amounting to $100 or more in a year. Other provisions included certain information about gifts, disclosure by category of value of information about property holdings, debts and interests in trades or businesses, and also disclosure of certain information about the finances of a spouse and dependent children. These disclosure requirements covered Congress and top Executive and Judicial branch employees and, to satisfy congressional sentiment that political opponents should, like incumbent Members, face mandatory disclosure, were extended to candidates for federal office. The Act provided that the designated Ethics Committees in the House and Senate should review all reports to see if they were properly and completely filed and required the Committees to notify any reporting individual who did not file an accurate report and give the individual an opportunity to correct it.

Limitations of the Ethics Codes

While the Nelson Committee Report on S. Res. 110 serves as a 'manual' to the Code of Conduct for the Senate, Representatives are provided with a separate Ethics Manual. However, it is left to Members to make their own judgment on what constitutes a 'conflict of interest'. This inevitably gives rise to ambiguity.

After surveying the 1979 financial disclosure reports, *Congressional Quarterly Weekly Report* (23.8.1980) commented on the confusion surrounding the financial disclosure requirements and warned that:

> The problems go beyond the structure of the forms. Both Houses and Senate ethics committees have issued advisory opinions which often blur the line between activities that are permissible and those which are not.

Some members have side-stepped the spirit of the disclosure provisions. For example, in 1980 many members listed trusts and partnerships in which they had interests but did not identify the nature of the trust or partnership business or its holdings. Another common practice was to list dividend income or liabilities arising from a stock or commodities brokerage firm without indicating from which stocks the dividend derived.

A further problem, as the Obey Commission had foreseen (H. Rept. 95–73) is that some Members have also attempted to evade the outside earned income limit. A survey of the 1979 financial disclosure reports reveals that with the impact of the then $8,743 limit, earned income dropped sharply in the House (it was not effective in the Senate) but then resurfaced as dividends, interest, capital gains and other forms of income not subject to the limit.

Other limitations of the codes arise not through ambiguity but through deliberate omissions in the codes themselves. In 1977 neither chamber was prepared to impose any new restrictions on Members serving on certain committees or voting in cases where their holdings or investments could pose a conflict of interest. Both chambers believed that any such restrictions which might prevent, for example, bankers sitting on the Banking Committee or members from farming areas sitting on the Agriculture Committee, would risk infringement of the legitimate representative function of Members. However, the avoidance of such restrictions contributes to the predicament observed by Kenneth Bradshaw and David Pring, that with less constitutional protection than his British counterpart, the Congressman is exposed to greater pressure.[6]

As a result of the committee structure of Congress a Congressman is expected to be a specialist in the areas of government which have been the subject of his legislative assignments. This facilitates the identification by interested pressure groups of the particular Congressman who could exert crucial influence on a bill or resolution. Through his committee membership he is also better placed than his British counterpart to influence the actions and decisions of agencies and Departments with whom his legislative assignments bring him into contact. An examination of honoraria paid to Members clearly indicates that interest groups do concentrate on Members who are in a position to help them promote their concerns. For example, in 1979 banking and credit union groups gave liberally to both the Senate Banking Committee (a total of $37,700 to seven members of this Committee) and the House Banking Committee, while farming and food organisations gave heavily to members of the House Agriculture Committee.[7]

A more general shortcoming of the codes is that the total financial worth of Members still cannot be ascertained because under the Ethics in Government Act, 1978 Members are required to disclose outside interests and holdings only within a range of dollar amounts. Also certain figures do not have to be reported. For example, Members do not have to furnish information on the value of travel and/or lodgings provided in connection with their honoraria for speeches. Also, the information required on holdings does not include certain types of blind trusts. Thus Senator Edward M. Kennedy (Democrat, Massachusetts), reputedly a wealthy man, found it possible to report his total holdings in 1982 as less than $10,000.[8]

The fundamental value of blind trusts as a means of avoiding conflict of interest is also debatable. We have already met this device in the context of the British House of Commons, whereby a Cabinet Minister who has shares in a concern closely connected with his own Department can place the holding in the hands of trustees in order to avoid the risk or suspicion of conflict of interest. The logic of the procedure is that once a Member's investments are put into a blind trust administered by private investment managers, he will thereafter be uncertain if he owns an interest in a concern which is effected by a decision of the legislature. However, as it is unlikely that the trustees would do other than retain profitable investments and manage the trust in the 'best interests' of their 'client', and these investments will revert back to the Member or Minister when he leaves public office, the effectiveness of blind trusts as tools in avoiding conflict of interest would seem open to question.

Perhaps the most fundamental limitation of the ethics codes is that they cannot guarantee ethical conduct. Witness, for example, the following cases of financial misconduct of one sort or another which have all occurred since the House and Senate embraced the new ethical safeguards: Senator Herman E. Talmadge (Democrat, Georgia) 'denounced' in 1979 for financial misconduct; Representative Charles C. Diggs Jr. (Democrat, Michigan) censured in 1979 for misuse of clerk hire funds; Representative Charles H. Wilson (Democrat, California) censured in 1980 for financial misconduct (the second time in two years he had been disciplined for accepting gifts in contravention of House Rules); Representative Michael 'Ozzie' Myers (Democrat, Pennsylvania) expelled from the House in October 1980 and seven other Members, including Senator Harrison A. Williams (Democrat, New Jersey), implicated in the Federal Bureau of Investigation's 'ABSCAM' political corruption probe.

The 'ABSCAM' case is not yet closed. In May 1983 the Supreme Court rejected the appeals by four members of the House accused on 'ABSCAM' bribery charges. Representatives Myers, Lederer and Murphy now face prison sentences of three years, and the fourth, Frank Thompson Jr. (Democrat, New Jersey) faces a 15 year sentence. Three other Members of Congress, including Senator Williams, are still working their way through the appeals system.

Congress has also suffered the embarrassment of the first ever indictment under the Ethics in Government Act, 1978. In April 1983 Representative George Hansen (Republican, Idaho) was indicted by a federal grand jury on the charge that he had failed on four counts to disclose certain financial activities as required under the 1978 law. The law provides a penalty of a maximum of five years' imprisonment and a $10,000 fine for each count. In June 1983 Hansen failed to clear himself of the charge, but won an indefinite postponement to allow him to appeal the ruling.

Trimming of the Ethics Codes

Despite these continuing cases of financial misconduct, there has been a gradual trimming away of the ethics codes in both Chambers since their initial passage. For example, the Senate code was amended in September 1977 to delay the effective date of financial disclosure and to loosen the restrictions written into the 1977 code on blind trusts (S. Res. 265). In 1979 it was further amended to delay the outside earned income limitation for four years until 1 January 1983 (S. Res. 93).

However, the main relaxation for both Chambers came in 1979 in the form of two resolutions (H. Res. 5 and S. Res. 220) which repealed the generally stricter financial disclosure rules of both Houses and replaced them with Title 1 of the Ethics in Government Act, 1978, as amended. This change did not affect other House or Senate Rules. The net effect of these changes was to make it more difficult for the electorate to assess the financial status and interests of their representatives.

It has been reported intermittently in *Congressional Quarterly* that both Chambers, encouraged by new chairmen heading their Ethics Committees, have been planning further revisions of their ethics codes, and recently there have been some striking departures from the spirit and letter of the 1977 reforms. In October 1981 Congress scrapped the total annual limit of $25,000 legitimate income from honoraria set by the 1976 Federal Election Law (PL 94–283), while retaining a separate provision of this law which limits the amount of each honorarium to $2,000. This change in the law did not affect Representatives, who are subject to the outside earned income limit rule, but *Congressional Quarterly* recorded that some Senators earned as much as $48,000 in honoraria that year. The Senate's outside earned income rule was due to become effective on 1 January 1980, but on 14 December 1982 with little debate Senators approved S. Res. 512 which deleted this rule from the Standing Rules of the Senate. In consequence, Senators could earn as much as they wished beyond their Senate salary by giving speeches, practising law or any other legal means.

Although Representatives retained their outside earned income rule, in December 1981 they had doubled the ceiling from 15 to 30 per cent ($18,200) of their official salary and had raised the cap on individual honoraria to $2,000. Moreover, as part of the deal reached in Conference on 19 December 1982, which had enabled Senators to scrap their income limit rule, Representatives for their part had taken the controversial step of giving themselves a 15 per cent ($9,100) pay rise to lift their salary to $69,800. Sensitive to public criticism over this rise, Representatives argued that Senators were getting the better financial deal because they could collect more in outside income than the size of the Representatives' rise.

In June 1983 the Senate voted to restore their salary to the same level as House Members ($69,800). Responding to public criticism they also voted to reinstate the as yet unused outside earned income limit rule. Both provisions were contained in the fiscal 1983 Supplemental Appropriations Bill (HR–3069–PL 98–63) passed by Congress in July 1983. The outside earned income rule, effective from 1 January 1984 limits the total annual amount of honoraria a senator may receive to 30 per cent of his salary ($20,940). Capping honoraria payments only, it is a laxer rule than that operating in the House, which prohibits members from keeping more than 30 per cent of their salaries from *all* outside earned income sources, not just honoraria.

Criticism of the income cap persists. Partly from those who wish to abolish it altogether, but also from those who argue it is creating a double standard to cap honoraria while not limiting unearned income. Condemning the new Senate income rule Senator John Tower (Republican, Texas) observed of the Senate, 'We have established a double standard, one that holds, I guess, that wealthy men are incorruptible but those of modest means are very corruptible indeed'.[9]

Lobby Disclosure Law Reform

Even the other side of the coin bears looking at since the perceived 'purchase' of influence through lobbying activities plays an increasing role in the operation of government. Whereas in Britain in 1969 the House of Commons Select Committee on the declaration of Members' interests judged the activities of lobbyists to be outside their terms of reference except to the extent that the personal pecuniary interests of Members were involved, Congress introduced legislation in 1946 to check the growing number of lobbies and pressure groups who sought to recruit the services of Congressmen. The Federal Regulation of Lobbying Act required all persons employed for the 'principal' purpose of lobbying to register with the Secretary of the Senate and the Clerk of the House and to file quarterly financial reports detailing their expenses. Organisations collecting money with the 'principal' intent of lobbying were also required to file details of their spending.

The Act is intended to provide Congress and the public with a record of how much money is spent by specific interest groups in order to exert influence on legislation. However, fundamental loopholes in the Act have developed which distort this picture. *Congressional Quarterly Weekly Report* (27.8.1983) illustrates the extent of the problem. In 1982 around 6,500 registered lobbyists reported spending approximately $35 million to promote, block or otherwise influence legislation in Congress, but some analysts of lobby spending estimate the true figure to be at least ten times higher than this.

One reason for this discrepancy is that lobbyists frequently fail to register the amount they spend in creating 'grass-roots' pressures in Congress. For example, when in early 1983 leading bankers masterminded a major lobby offensive against the withholding of taxes on interests and dividends, the financial industry groups heading the campaign registered spending around $500,000 to exert pressure on Congress. Their lobby reports did not include their expenditure on the distribution of anti-withholding propaganda to individual banks. A more fundamental problem, not envisaged by Congress in 1946, derives from the wording of the Act itself: many organisations who have clear legislative interests but do not describe themselves as 'principally' concerned with lobbying simply exempt themselves from the terms of the Act.

Periodic attempts by the House or the Senate to broaden the scope of the lobby disclosure law or to tighten its provisions have failed. In 1976 both Chambers approved lobby disclosure provisions but were then unable to overcome the differences between the two versions. Again in 1978 the House voted for a tougher lobby disclosure law but this languished in the Senate. The failure to gain congressional agreement to lobby reform legislation was taken to be a personal set-back for President Carter who had shown a keen interest in the problem. In a message to Congress in January 1980 he had said:

> The American people have a right to know what significant influences affect their national legislature . . . The proliferation of well-financed organizational lobbying activities during recent years has demonstrated the clear need for reform of the outdated and ineffective lobby disclosure law now in effect.[10]

It has been suggested that the more recent reluctance to grasp the nettle of the lobbying issue is symptomatic of the deregulatory climate associated with the Reagan Administration. A more serious manifestation of this climate is the bill Senator Dave Durenberger (Republican, Minnesota) is reported to be planning to introduce in mid-1984. Far from tightening the lobby disclosure law, this bill would in effect repeal the provisions of the 1946 Act and abolish altogether the mandatory requirement for lobbyists to register and file their expenses.

Problems of Self-Discipline

The gradual trimming to the ethics codes and the question mark that hangs over the future existence of the lobbying law are manifestations of the problem of congressional self-discipline. The constitutional requirement that Congress discipline itself was intended to shield each House from improper interference from the judicial and executive branches of Government. However, it also adds to Congress's difficulties in dealing with ethical issues. In part, Members' motivation to deal with ethical issues tends to be low, ranging from an unwillingness to initiate reforms without the stimulus of scandals and consequent press criticism, to outright opposition (for example, the Laxalt court case).

Additionally, once rules are introduced the problems of enforcement and policing arise. Reporting in March 1981 (FPCD–81–20), the General Accounting Office concluded that the House and Senate needed to be more effective both in identifying everyone required to file a disclosure statement and in checking the fullness and accuracy of the information once filed. The GAO was particularly concerned over Congress's failure adequately to police blind trusts, set up by members in order to divorce their official actions from their private holdings, as it had found that sixteen of the twenty blind trusts approved by the Congressional Ethics Committees did not fulfil the legal requirement for such trusts.

Even finding members for these Ethics Committees has not been easy. Members are unwilling to sit in judgment on colleagues or to swear a formal complaint against colleagues. Also expulsion, the ultimate penalty, is difficult to impose because it requires a two-thirds majority vote. Voter apathy too has played a part in Congress's inaction on charges of misconduct, with Members who have been charged with unethical activities finding that their constituents are nevertheless ready to re-elect them.

Finally, in pursuit of ethical conduct Congress has had to take into account competing and often conflicting goals such as Members' morale and recruitment. In reality many Congressmen share the view of the member of the House Rules Committee who said of the 1977 ethics reforms:

> What we are doing is creating a situation which means that good, qualified, able, capable people are going to avoid public service of this type like the plague. Why should they jeopardize their family and their kids, their income and everything else for a 2-year situation?[11]

Sentiments such as these impede serious application of restraints on conflict of interest.

9 A Problem of Interest

The main concern of this book has been with the dilemma of conflict of interest in representative democracies. Throughout it is evident that conflict of interest is not in itself an *act* of wrongdoing. It is a *situation* which might raise questions of improper motives, whereby an official has a direct or indirect private financial interest which might influence, or appear to influence, the performance of his public duties and responsibilities. Though allegations of conflict of interest frequently slide into accusations of corruption in the heat of a political scandal, the two are not synonymous. Conflict of interest does not necessarily imply resolution in favour of personal advantage or benefit, or to the advantage of those offering inducements, simply that a conflict exists. Corruption on the other hand can be viewed as a particular method of resolving this conflict, whereby personal financial interest or gain actually distorts the exercise of an official's public duties and responsibilities. Corruption is not an end in itself, rather an illegal *means* of effecting a particular outcome.

The focus of this study of conflict of interest has been the legislative branch of politics where embarrassing revelations have increasingly forced legislatures to reflect on putting their own houses in order. In particular we have examined the experiences of the British House of Commons and, to a lesser extent, the American Congress in grappling with the problem. We can now bring together and summarise the particular factors which impinge on the conflict of interest dilemma and which need to be taken into account in formulating conflict of interest restraints for elected officials. We can also evaluate and comment on the different approaches that have been adopted.

Regulating Conflict of Interest: A Reappraisal

It is the representative dimension of the legislator's role and the special features of legislative employment that fundamentally differentiate the problem of conflict of interest in legislatures from that in the executive branch. As we have seen, not only do these characteristics create the difficulty of distinguishing between a legitimate representation of interests and an improper conflict of interest, they also mean that certain conflicts are inherent in the political system as currently constituted and are not necessarily harmful or immoral; for example, where the Member's interest coincides with that of his constituents and he risks the appearance of his fiduciary duties conflicting with his public responsibilities. Where this type of conflict occurs or appears to occur prudence should be exercised, and the emphasis must remain on the Member's fiduciary obligations. However, there is a strong case for arguing that proposals designed actually to eliminate such conflicts or their appearance are probably misguided and may in fact compromise a Member's ability to perform his representative role effectively.[1]

Then there is the broad and somewhat intangible matter of the social, economic and political context from which individuals are recruited and in which they operate. For practical reasons conflict of interest restraints are usually restricted to economic ties. Nevertheless, the different social contexts and experiences of Members largely determine what interests and behaviour are considered relevant to the conflict of interest debate. The type of individual attracted by, and eventually elected or appointed to the legislature partially defines the conflict of interest problem. The nature and extent of Members' personal financial holdings and involvements largely determine the range of possible conflicts. So does the political and moral climate in which the representative functions, and the prevailing attitude towards outside interests and employment. Until recently neither Parliament nor Congress thought it necessary to restrict the outside employment of Members, preferring to emphasise disclosure of interests rather than their avoidance. The concept of representation in a more colloquial sense has significance here too. As one Conservative Member of the British Parliament pointed out to me, to get a completely 'sanitised' MP devoid of all interests would be as ridiculous as it would be impossible; and in any case, such an MP would then not be 'representative' of the majority of his constituents.

The delicate and difficult task of balancing the target of avoiding conflict of interest with the competing goals of Members' recruitment and morale is evident in both the British and the American experience. A further balance has to be struck between a Member's need for privacy and the public interest in the disclosure of some interests. Whether a Member is entitled to the same degree of privacy as an ordinary citizen, or whether involvement in public life should entail the acceptance of an erosion of personal privacy is a matter for debate. The prevailing attitude on this issue will substantially determine the nature and stringency of conflict of interest provisions. Inevitably these provisions will be a compromise formula, giving the 'appropriate' amount of information about interests relevant to a Member's parliamentary action and behaviour, while at the same time protecting his privacy in other aspects of life. As we have seen, it is inevitable that there be competing and conflicting views, both on what level of disclosure is appropriate, and on the scope of interests that influence a Member in the performance of his parliamentary duties.

The status that Members ascribe to themselves in political life is also an essential factor to be taken into account. It is evident that the extent to which Members consider themselves to be, and are expected by others to be, full-time or part-time Members of an assembly influences their attitudes towards the possession of outside interests and/or employment. The extent to which the job of a Member is seen as either part-time or full-time also influences the fixing of the level of remuneration. Although the fact is often unintentionally or deliberately overlooked, the level of salary and attendant allowances (for example, for secretarial help and research, travel, subsistence, post and telephone) influences the tendency for Members to retain or take up outside employment and interests; as does the insecurity and uncertainty of elected office. These factors also affect the recruitment of prospective candidates. The services and facilities available or denied to Members, such as information and research for example, likewise influence the type and extent of Members' involvement with outside interests. Recently in Britain the employment of research assistants who are paid employees of lobbying companies or consultancies has also opened up scope for improper access by these organisations to MPs, Ministers and parliamentary documents.

Elected members are justifiably concerned about their long-term security, and if limits and prohibitions are to be placed on their outside interests and employment, then it will be necessary to fix a salary level which is sufficient to enable and encourage compliance with these restrictions. As we saw in chapter 3, however, improvements in salary level and tenure (for example, pension schemes and severance pay) do not necessarily guarantee protection against conflict of interest. It is also an unfortunate fact that even the practice of MPs and Congressmen receiving a public salary itself attracts a unique form of conflict of interest. Members' personal economic interests in determining their own salaries currently creates an unavoidable conflict of interest to which Parliament and Congress are highly sensitive.

In ascertaining the requirements of conflict of interest restraints it is also necessary to have some idea of where the opportunities for conflict of interest arise for the Member in the performance of his public duties and responsibilities. This will vary from country to country depending on the constitutional arrangements of the political system. For example, in the parliamentary system of government in Britain an individual MP who is not also a minister and therefore part of the Executive has limited opportunities for influencing public policy. Nevertheless, we have seen that conflict of interest provisions have to acknowledge that MPs do have the facility of access to people of influence, particularly Ministers, and that opportunities do exist for promoting outside interest on the floor of the House or in Committees.

Different legislatures have different functions and methods of procedure, and will make different demands on their Members. This diversity makes institutional comparisons difficult because it is hard to compare like with like. Conflict of interest proposals need to be tailored to suit the role and activities of Members in a particular legislative system, but this does not necessarily entail an insular approach. Much can be learnt from the practices and experiences of other countries. Britain, for example, may have something to learn from the American Federal Regulation of Lobbying Act, despite its faults. Up until now the British Parliament has avoided interfering with the activity of lobbyists except to the extent that the personal pecuniary interests of Members were involved. This attitude may to some extent derive from a belief that the increasing interpenetration of government and industry, which has brought private business organisations increasingly under the umbrella of the machinery of government and administration, has diminished the political importance of the individual Member in the promotion of interests. However, it is just as plausible that such 'interpenetration' has actually *widened* the scope of the political agenda to include new issues upon which MPs (as well as Departments and Ministers) can be profitably lobbied. There is an increasingly strong case for similar regulation and registration of lobbyists in Britain as is required under the Lobbying Act in America. Currently the Select Committee on Members' Interests is conducting an urgent inquiry into parliamentary lobbyists. The character of its recommendations remains to be seen.

Finally, conflict of interest restraints have to be complied with if they are to achieve their objectives: namely, in the long term to maintain the actuality and appearance of a high standard of ethical conduct in the public service; and more immediately, to enable the individual to separate his legitimate interests from his public duty, and to avoid connections or associations which raise questions of improper motives. Proposals must, therefore, include consideration of the machinery for policing and enforcing the provisions. Sensitive questions arise here concerning the appropriate forum and procedures for adjudicating upon conflicts of interest on the part of elected representatives, although the final solution will be determined largely by the constitutional arrangements of the country concerned. The fundamental issue at stake is whether the legislature itself should have the sole right to regulate and adjudicate upon the conduct of its Members in their representative capacity – as is traditionally the case with the British House of Commons – or whether this responsibility should be transferred to some other body, for example, a judicial forum in the courts.

Modus Operandi: Alternative Approaches

These constituents of the conflict of interest debate are not static and their character will also vary according to different political traditions and constitutional arrangements. Diverse political systems create different opportunities for conflict of interest and adopt different approaches to the problem.

The focus of our investigation has been the British House of Commons and we have seen that in ethical matters a distinguishing factor has been its essentially *ad hoc* response to the problem of conflict of interest. The mood of self-criticism of the House tends to ebb and flow, but the traditional belief in the expediency of outside interests remains deep-rooted. In the absence of strong outside stimuli, the House has shown itself reluctant to interfere with Members' outside financial interests.

As a result, it has evolved a distinctive approach to handling the problem of conflict of interest among legislators. Characterised by a reliance on parliamentary tradition and a minimum of written rules, the British prescription believes the individual Member to be the best judge in avoiding conflict of interest situations. The emphasis is on disclosure of interests and the House has rarely found it necessary to restrict the outside interests or employment of Members.

Conflict of interest regulation has taken the form of a series of loosely connected exercises in self-discipline. The 'issue-attention cycle' model, describing a systematic cycle of exposed wrongdoing, increasing public interest and then growing boredom with the problem of conflict of interest summarises the pattern of the House's response. It emphasises criteria such as Members' indiscretions, public and parliamentary anxiety and governmental tactics. However, the operation and eventual outcome of each 'issue-attention cycle' cannot be understood and explained in isolation from the beliefs and values which shape Members' attitudes towards conflict of interest. There is a reciprocal process. Such predispositions and assumptions underlie Members' reactions to contemporary incidents and account for the genuine differences of opinion among Members as to what action by the House, if any, is appropriate at each stage of the cycle. In turn, environmental situations, for example the Bagier affair and the Poulson scandal, give rise to changes in the beliefs and values and habits of thought which guide and inform Members' action and behaviour.

Many of these values and beliefs have been identified in this study as historical residues of a political culture born out of the aristocratic tradition in government. They have a common source as characteristics of a phenomenon in English culture often referred to as the 'gentleman ethic'. With a strong base in the customs and traditions of the House (embodied to some extent in parliamentary privilege) the values of honour, self-restraint, loyalty and mutual trust have encouraged constitutional reliance on ethical restraints and integrity, on human character, discretion and internalised psychological checks in the regulation of Members' interests, rather than on codes of conduct or written law. The 'amateur ideal', though no longer uncontested, still provides for many present day parliamentarians a subconscious standard for their actions and prescribes their proper role. This tradition is closely allied with the notion of part-time membership of Parliament and stands opposed to a trend towards the full-time, 'professional' MP. The extent to which MPs view themselves as full-time or part-time Members in turn influences their attitudes towards Members' pay and outside interests.

The major intra- and inter-party differences towards conflict of interest restraints are due largely to different underlying predispositions on the part of Members towards these fundamental values or beliefs. While indicating some shifts in intra- and inter-party opinion, my study suggests that even though MPs are now more highly paid and are increasingly becoming full-time Members because of the pressure of parliamentary work, residues of the 'gentleman ethic' do still provide a pattern and example for many MPs in their approach towards the regulation of outside interests. It is not essential to my argument that they perceive or describe their behaviour in these terms. As Ronald Fletcher has observed:

> How many of us know the origins and many developments from cumulative contributions of generations of men in the immemorial past of our society of the games we play, the skills we use, the values we stand by, the beliefs we adopt, the rituals we find meaningful and moving? It is on the face of it, a strange thing, that no one person, not one group, not one entire generation alive at any one time, can fully know the many dimensions of culture which

> are active in the ways of life they lead. Just as there are unforeseen consequences for the future of men's actions now, so there are unforeseen consequences from the past, active within them, which are equally important.[2]

The codified response of the American Congress in recent years highlights the uniquely British experience of the House of Commons, and illustrates an alternative approach to conflict of interest regulation. My study has demonstrated the many shifting attitudes towards the regulation of elected members' interests, but fundamentally these boil down to two opposing points or view or emphases: on the one hand there is the argument for minimal rules and reliance on mutual trust and individual integrity, prominent in Britain; and on the other hand there is the view, evident in post-Watergate America, that codification of rules and perhaps even the introduction of legislation is necessary. Each solution carries with it a combination of 'costs' in terms of the potential loss of other values and these have been discussed and illustrated in earlier chapters. The two positions can be summarised in ideal type form as follows; in practice they are not mutually exclusive.

The minimal rules solution emphasises the spirit of disclosure and the preservation of tradition. Reliance is placed on the honour and integrity of the individual and the mutual trust of the collectivity. The privacy of the individual is revered and he or she is entrusted with the discretion to judge what interests should be disclosed. The 'costs' of this approach are in terms of lack of guidance, clarity and certainty. The differential perception of Members as to what should be disclosed or what is unacceptable conduct is a perennial problem, rules or no rules, but is more likely to flourish where guidance is lacking. The corollary of the preservation of privacy is the lack of publicly available information on Members' pecuniary interests which provides a potential breeding ground for suspicion and allegations, often unfounded, of conflict of interest.

The solution which emphasises codification and possibily legislation aims to introduce greater clarity and certainty into the regulation of Members' interests. Public confidence is expected to be increased, depending on the effectiveness of the codification adopted, because the elected assembly is *seen* to be regulating Members' interests. Members themselves are provided with a guide as to what standard of conduct is required. However, this solution is likely to involve 'costs' in terms of some erosion of privacy, spirit of disclosure, flexibility and discretion and of values such as honour, mutual trust and so on. If regulation of Members' interests is imposed by statute then the courts become involved and for parliamentary systems such as in Britain, this would mean a consequent erosion of parliamentary sovereignty.

As we have seen, the American Congress has been pushed further down the path to codification than the British House of Commons. The tremors from the Watergate affair widened cracks in the complacency surrounding standards of conduct in government and swayed opinion towards conflict of interest legislation. The 1978 Ethics in Government Act codified the disclosure requirements for Congress and senior executive and judicial branch employees and enabled civil penalties – in particular fines – to be imposed for wilful violations.

In Britain codes of ethics and committees charged with their enforcement are generally associated with the professions, and as the late Richard Crossman observed in 1972, 'politicians have never regarded Parliament as a profession with its own code of ethics'.[3] However, there are signs that this attitude might be changing, albeit slowly and cautiously. The 1974 Resolutions concerning declaration and registration of interests can be seen as a first step towards the codification solution. Although the Register of Members' Interests may be judged a failure in terms of guaranteeing accurate and comprehensive information about Members' financial interests, at the very least its existence and the periodic debates and parliamentary questions associated with it, contribute towards providing MPs with some guidance as to what interests they should keep separate from their public duties and be prepared to disclose. It requires an MP to disclose all relevant interests or to take a conscious decision to conceal them, and if he takes that decision he will know that he is abusing his position.

Some conflicts of interest are endemic in systems of representative government and members' opinions will always differ on what constitutes an improper conflict, but this does not mean that we should abandon altogether attempts to provide relatively unambiguous guidelines and safeguards. In earlier chapters I have made other recommendations for conflict of interest reform which would propel the House of Commons further towards the codification solution. In brief, these include: further consideration to be given to improving and tightening the categories of registrable interests (for example, a requirement for MPs to list the *amount* they receive as fees from lobbyists), and clearer guidelines concerning the interests of relatives; a consolidation of the *ad hoc* rules and conventions of parliamentary etiquette into a coherent code prescribing and circumscribing the conduct of MPs, and to be brought to the attention of every MP; a review of MPs' status under the Prevention of Corruption Acts; and serious consideration given to the introduction of legislation to register and regulate the activities of parliamentary lobbyists.

My impression is that a further possible option of raising parliamentary salaries and banning outside interests and employment would not be workable without a considerable shift in the traditional attitudes and prejudices of MPs. As an alternative to this, it has been suggested elsewhere[4] that the answer lies in applying to MPs a code similar to that regulating local government councillors; that an MP should not just be required to declare his outside interests but should then be disallowed from speaking, voting or in any other way using his elective office to further that interest. Given the increasingly complex relationship between government and society, this recommendation for reform would also seem to be unrealistic. The increasing association of MPs with interest groups that seek to influence the process of government has become an integral part of both the British and the American political system. It is acceptable, even where financial considerations are involved, so long as the connection is known and the MP's role is advisory and not one of advocating in the House interests in which he may have a financial connection.

Neither the British House of Commons nor the American Congress necessarily provide the blueprint for other countries to follow in dealing with conflict of interest, but they do provide insight into the problems and prejudices that are likely to be encountered in tackling the problem. In the final analysis, as the American experience illustrates, even the most stringent of financial ethics codes is difficult to enforce and cannot ensure ethical behaviour. Whether we look at established systems of representative government or small emerging nations, inevitably individual responsibility and integrity, whether nurtured or tested by the prevailing morality of society, have to be the mainspring of a public service ethic. Nevertheless, external controls in the form of ethics codes, financial disclosure provisions and income limitations have become a necessary and secondary support system, if only to sharpen the moral judgments of those who know that against such controls their actions can be challenged.

Notes and References

1 Introduction: Studying Conflict of Interest

1 'The Conflict of Interest Issue in the British House of Commons: a Practical Problem and a Conceptual Conundrum'. Ph.D. thesis, University of London, November 1982.
2 See Appendix 1: A Note on Sources and Appendix 2: A Note on Interview Technique.
3 Michael Rush and Malcolm Shaw (eds), *The House of Commons: Services and Facilities*, London, George Allen and Unwin Ltd, 1974, pp. 252–4.
4 By 'normative theory' is meant 'a systematic explanation of values or ideals, including the reasons why they are held, the effects they may have on behaviour, their interrelationship with other values, etc. A normative theory may also seek to provide grounds for the prescription of values, e.g. Marxist theory or democratic theory'. By 'empiricism' is meant 'the belief that experienced phenomenon, rather than theories or ideas, are the basis of knowledge, and that at best, only those hypotheses, theories and scientific laws which are validated by observable experience should be included in the body of accepted knowledge within a discipline'. Both definitions are taken from Geoffrey K. Roberts, *A Dictionary of Political Analysis*, London, Longman, 1971, pp. 135, 74.
5 Max Weber, *Methodology of the Social Sciences*, translated and edited by Edward A. Shils and Henry A. Finch, New York, The Free Press, 1949: essay on '"Objectivity" in Social Sciences and Social Policy', pp. 49–112.

6 This term and the ensuing argument against reifying culture as an independent variable are based on the approach taken by Barrington Moore Jr. in *Social Origins of Dictatorship and Democracy*, Great Britain, Penguin University Books, 1973, pp. 485–7.
7 Fred Greenstein, *Personality and Politics*, Chicago, Markham Publishing Co, 1969, p. 7.
8 Ibid., p. 29.
9 In recognising the importance of historical residues, as opposed to functional considerations, as factors in explanation I was encouraged by V. Subramaniam's explanation of the present position of the specialist in different countries on the basis of their historical and political evolution in the last two centuries: 'The relative status of specialists and generalists: an attempt at a comparative historical explanation', *Public Administration*, Vol. 46 (1968), pp. 331–40.
10 No attempt is made here to trace the historical emergence of the gentleman ethic and its entrenchment in the House of Commons. The interested reader is referred to the thesis, lodged at the University of London Library, on which this book is based.
11 For an early example see Anthony Downs, 'Up and down with ecology – the "issue-attention cycle"', *The Public Interest*, No. 26, Winter 1972.
12 See for example J.J. Richardson and A.G. Jordan, *Governing Under Pressure: the Policy Process in a Post-Parliamentary Democracy*, London, Martin Robertson, 1979, particularly Ch. 4, 'The Emergence of Issues and Policies'.
13 Steven Lukes, *Power: A Radical View*, London, The Macmillan Press Ltd, 1974, especially Ch. 3, 'The Two Dimensional View'. A classical contribution to this view is Peter Bachrach and Morton S. Baratz, 'The two faces of power', *American Political Science Review*, 56 (1962), pp. 947–52.
14 Anthony Downs, loc. cit., p. 39.
15 Francis E. Rourke, 'The United States' in Itzhak Galnor (ed), *Government Secrecy in Democracies*, New York, New York University Press, 1977, p. 113.

2 The Problem of Conflict of Interest in Representative Democracies

1 James C. Kirby Jr., *Congress and the Public Trust*, Report of the Association of the Bar of the City of New York Special Committee on Congressional Ethics, New York, Atheneum, 1971, p. 42, citing the Association of the Bar of the City of New York, *Conflict of Interest and Federal Service*, 1960, p. 17.

2 Robert S. Getz, *Congressional Ethics. The Conflict of Interest Issue*, USA, D. Van Nostrand Co Ltd, 1966, p. 4.
3 Cornelius O'Leary, *The Elimination of Corrupt Practices in British Elections 1868–1911*, Oxford at the Clarendon Press, 1962, p. 232.
4 E.E. Schattschneider, *The Semi-Sovereign People*, New York, Holt, Rinehart and Winston, 1960, pp. 24–25.
5 Steven Lukes, op. cit., p. 34.
6 Samuel E., Finer, *Anonymous Empire. A Study of the Lobby in Great Britain*, London, Pall Mall Press, rev. ed. 1969, p. 108.
7 George W. Jones, 'Corruption and the Public Interest', *New Society*, Vol. 25, No. 572 (20 Sept 1973), pp. 703–5.
8 Benjamin Disraeli, *Whigs and Whiggism*, ed. William Hutcheon, London, 1913, 'The Letters of Runnymede', p. 249.
9 For example, Heinz Eulau et al., 'The Role of the Representative', *American Political Science Review*, LIII (Sept 1959).
10 Hanna Fenichel Pitkin, *The Concept of Representation*, USA, University of California Press, 1972, p. 4.
11 Eulau, loc. cit., p. 745.
12 Pitkin, op. cit., p. 218.
13 J.D. Stewart, *British Pressure Groups: Their Role in Relation to the House of Commons*, Oxford & New York, 1958.
14 For example, used by J.S. Nye, 'Corruption and Political Development: A Cost-Benefit Analysis' in Arnold J. Heidenheimer, *Political Corruption: Readings in Comparative Analysis*, New York, Holt, Rinehart and Winston Inc, 1970, pp. 564–78.
15 For example, used by Jacob van Klavern, 'The Concept of Corruption', in Heidenheimer, op. cit., pp. 38–41.
16 For example, used by Carl J. Friedrich, 'Political Pathology', *Political Quarterly*, No. 37 (1966), p. 74.
17 Pitkin, op. cit., p. 167.
18 S. Chibnal and P. Saunders, 'Worlds Apart: Notes on the Social Reality of Corruption', *British Journal of Sociology*, 28 (1977).
19 Thurman Arnold, 'US Congress Senate, Committee on Labour and Public Welfare', 1951. Establishment of a Commission on Ethics in Government: hearings before a sub-committee to study Senate Concurrent Resolution 21 of the Committee on Labour and Public Welfare. Eighty-second Congress, 1st Session, Washington, Government Printing Office, p. 372.

3 The Tradition of the Financially Independent Member

1 For example, see J.F.S. Ross, *Parliamentary Representation*, London, Eyre and Spottiswoode, 2nd ed. 1948; J.F.S. Ross, *Elections*

and Electors, London, Eyre and Spottiswoode, 1955; *The Times Guide to the House of Commons*, London, Times Books Ltd: the June 1983 edition is the latest in a series which began in 1880; Andrew Roth, *The Business Background of MPs*: editions have appeared in 1961, 1963, 1965, 1967, 1972, 1975/6, all published in London by Parliamentary Profiles Services Ltd; Colin Mellors, *The British MP. A Socio-Economic Study of the House of Commons*, England, Saxon House, 1978.

2 W. L. Guttsman, *The British Political Elite*, London, MacGibbon and Key, rev. ed. 1965, p. 29.

3 V. Subramaniam, loc. cit., pp. 331–40.

4 Swift, 'Letter of Pope', 10 January 1721; cited in Edward and Annie Porritt, *The Unreformed House of Commons: Parliamentary Representation Before 1832*, Cambridge, 1909, Vol. 1, p. 170.

5 Figures derived from Gerritt P. Judd, *Members of Parliament 1734–1832*, New Haven, 1955.

6 Peter Alfred Taylor MP, 'Payment of Members', Pamphlets, London, Trubner & Co., 1870.

7 Samuel H. Beer, 'The Representation of Interests in British Government: Historical Background', *American Political Science Review*, Vol. LI (1957), pp. 613–50.

8 Cited by Beer, ibid., p. 622.

9 Joseph Redlich, *The Procedure of the House of Commons*, trans. E.A. Steinthal, Archibald, Constable and Co. Ltd, 1908, Vol. II, p. 116.

10 J.F.S. Ross, 1948, op. cit., p. 138.

11 Peter G. Richards, 'MPs' Pay', pp. 95–101, in J.P. Mackintosh (ed), *Parliament and People*, England, Saxon House, 1978.

12 Michael Rush, 'Members' Salaries, Allowances, Pensions and Related Facilities', pp. 112–26, in Michael Rush (ed), *The House of Commons: Services and Facilities, 1972–1982*, London, Policy Studies Institute No. 614, 1983.

13 In June 1984 the Leader of the Commons, Mr. John Biffen, announced a scheme for wider pension rights for MPs, with possible eligibility below the 62 year age limit. The move followed protests from both sides of the House over hardship cases involving long-serving MPs who lost their seats just short of pensionable age.

14 It would seem that when the linkage to civil service pay was made there were only two grades which were then receiving a salary of £18,500, and both ranks are disappearing in civil service reorganisation.

15 The actual percentage of Members pursuing some kind of regular or occasional employment was 70 per cent. This figure is the same as that emerging from the survey conducted by the Boyle Commission in 1971. While the two findings cannot be directly compared, they do suggest that it is likely that the proportion of MPs pursuing some kind of outside employment remained fairly constant between 1971 and

1974. However, the figures reveal nothing about the *time* spent on such employment, which might have changed.

4 The Tradition of the Honourable Member

1 Sir Thomas Erskine May, *Parliamentary Practice*, London, Butterworths; first published in 1844 and now in its nineteenth edition, 1976, p. 67. Hereafter referred to as *Erskine May* 19 ed.
2 Redlich, op. cit., Vol. 1, p. 46.
3 These are the organisational categories under which G. Marshall surveys the application of privileges in the twentieth century. Inevitably they overlap; Geoffrey Marshall, 'The House of Commons and its Privileges' in S.A. Walkland (ed), *The House of Commons in the Twentieth Century*, Oxford, Clarendon, 1979.
4 *Erskine May* 19 ed., p. 68. See also *Halsbury's Laws of England*, 3rd ed., Vol. 28, p. 464.
5 Geoffrey Marshall, op. cit., p. 228.
6 Barry McGill, 'Conflicts of Interest: English Experience 1782–1914', *Western Political Quarterly*, Vol. XII (1959), pp. 825–26.
7 O. Cyprian Williams, *The Historical Development of Private Bill Procedure and Standing Orders of the House of Commons*, London, HMSO, 1948, Vol. 1, p. 30 and note 1.
8 These principles are discussed in *Members of Parliament and Conflicts of Interests*, Green Paper signed by the President of the Privy Council of the Canadian Parliament, July 1973, p. 10.
9 Note by the Secretary of the Cabinet, 22 October 1947, PRO ref: Prem 8/629.
10 Redlich, op. cit., Vol. II, p. 128.

5 To Be A Gentleman Is Not Enough: The Register

1 Richard Crossman, *The Diaries of a Cabinet Minister*, Vol. 3, London, Hamish Hamilton and Jonathan Cape, 1977, p. 406. It was the publication of the Crossman Diaries that led to the setting up of the Committee of Privy Counsellors on Ministerial Memoirs (*Radcliffe Report*, Cmnd 6386:1976) to consider what rules should govern the publication by former Ministers of memoirs and other works relating to their experiences as Ministers.
2 The Liberal Party believed a register could be established without an Act of Parliament. Consequently, in June 1967, they established a voluntary open register of Liberal MPs' interests, subject to revision every six months.

3 Although Mr. Hamilton exploited the early termination of business on 4 August 1972 to raise the matter of Members' expenses and financial interests on the adjournment. Even then, over half the time was devoted to consideration of the Boyle Committee's recommendations for a travel grant fund for MPs. (*HC Debs* 842:1972, 1176–1222).

4 For a more general commentary see, for example, Martin Tomkinson, *Guide to the Poulson Case*, Private Eye Extra, London, Pressdram Ltd, 1973. The Salmon Commission (Cmnd 6524) also provides a useful summary of the case.

5 See Ray Fitzwalter, 'Breaking the Poulson Story', *New Statesman*, 4 May 1973, pp. 652–3.

6 Mr. Poulson's connection with the Maudling family had already been investigated by *Private Eye*, but did not receive wider circulation until the commencement of the bankruptcy proceedings. *Private Eye* had also made much of Mr. Maudling's previous involvement with an off-shore trust, Real Estate of America.

7 The three MPs named were the late Sir Herbert Butcher (Nat Lib), Mr. John Cordle (Cons) and Mr. Albert Roberts (Lab). During the course of the bankruptcy hearings the name of the late Mr. Anthony Crosland (Lab) was also mentioned in connection with the acceptance of a silver coffee pot from Poulson, alleged to be worth £500. He announced he would send the pot to the Official Receiver in Bankruptcy, *The Times*, 19.3.1973.

8 Former Under-Secretary in charge of Agriculture at the Scottish Office. Seconded in 1959 to assist (Lord) Hugh Fraser with the Aviemore Centre in the Scottish Highlands. Acted as liaison officer between the developers and the Government.

9 In evidence to the Salmon Commission the Attorney General stated that: 'A substantial part of the Poulson investigation has been taken up with investigating allegations against Members of Parliament'. PRO Ref. Ho. 241/9. Although no MPs were prosecuted – MPs are not covered by the criminal law in respect of corruption and bribery in their capacity as MPs – a select committee was eventually set up in November 1976 to inquire into the conduct of Members in connection with the affairs of Poulson (*HC* 490: 1976/7).

10 This affair involved disclosure of payments of Lonrho's funds by the Company's chief executive 'Tiny' Rowland, as gifts, rewards and inducements in connection with the group's overseas business (mainly in Africa). It was revealed in 1971 that Rowland had personally appointed a Conservative MP, the Rt. Hon. Duncan Sandys, as consultant to the company on a fee-paying basis. This consultancy was kept secret, and on learning that it had not been sanctioned by the Board of Directors of Lonrho, Duncan Sandys gave up his contract and returned

the fee. As a result of these disclosures Mr. Edward Heath made his speech in the House about 'the unpleasant and unacceptable face of capitalism' (*HC Debs* 856:1973, 1243).

11 Pressure from Labour backbenchers on the PLP, early in the 1970–1974 Parliament, to look at the problem of outside interests led to the formation of a joint front and backbench committee on 27 July 1972, chaired by the Deputy Leader, Mr. Short. Information about this committee was obtained from the Assistant Secretary of the PLP.

12 The Royal Commission, chaired by Lord Salmon, reported in 1976 (Cmnd 6524).

13 For an account of Mr. Short's connection with Mr. T. Dan Smith see Report from the Select Committee on Conduct of Members, *HC* 490: 1976/7, paras 9–11.

14 Over 80 per cent of my sample survey of Members insisted that in general the conduct of the House could still be described as amateur. However, the sample survey also revealed a distinct lack of agreement among Members as to what they understood by the terms 'amateurism' and 'professionalism' in a parliamentary context.

15 See chapter 8, p. 149.

16 Although a Speaker's Conference has frequently been promised, this issue has not so far been dealt with. The Clerk to the Committee concludes that a formidable array of problems await the Conference so it must be doubtful that this recommendation will be put into effect. C.B. Winnifrith, 'Members' Interests', *The Table*, Vol. XLIII (1975), pp. 30–35.

17 Quoted in the *Sunday Times*, 30.11.1975.

6 The House of Commons and Internal Discipline

1 An annotated table of complaints referred to the Committee of Privileges since 1945 is appended to the Third Report from the Committee of Privileges, *HC* 417: 1976–7, Appendix C.

2 For a discussion of these problems see for example George W. Keeton, *Trial by Tribunal*, London, Museum Press Ltd, 1960.

3 The Study of Parliament Group was formed in 1963 and comprises academics and officers of the Houses of Parliament. It works largely through small study groups and undertakes parliamentary research.

4 The Prevention of Corruption Acts include: Public Bodies Corrupt Practices Act, 1889 (*Halsbury's Statutes of England*, 2nd ed., Vol. 5, pp. 919–21); The Prevention of Corruption Act, 1906 (Ibid., pp. 924–5); The Prevention of Corruption Act, 1916 (Ibid., pp. 1043–4). For a summary of these Acts see the *Report of the Salmon Commission* (Cmnd 6524:1976).

5 Letter to *The Times*, 5.11.1976.
6 Graham Zellick, 'Bribery of Members of Parliament and the Criminal Law', *Public Law*, Spring 1979, pp. 31–58.
7 For example see *R. v White* (1875) 13 S.C.R. (N.S.W.) (L) 322; *R. v Boston* (1923) 33 C.L.R. 386, 400.
8 *R. v Boston*, op. cit., p. 412.
9 Zellick, loc. cit., p. 53.
10 C.J. Boulton, 'Conduct of Members', *The Table*, Vol. XLVI (1978), p. 31.
11 R. Boothby, *Boothby: Recollections of a Rebel*, Hutchinson, 1978, p. 172.
12 *Observer*, 29.10.1978.
13 John Wilkes (1727–1797), MP for Aylesbury and subsequently Middlesex, vindicated the right of the electorate to return the candidate of their choice to House of Commons.
14 Mr. Enoch Powell (UUUC), Mr. Alex Lyon (Lab), Revd. Ian Paisley (UU), Mr. Kenneth Lewis (Con), Sir John Langford-Holt (Con).
15 *HC* 249: 20 March 1981; *HC* 158: 18 January 1982; *HC* 172: 17 January 1983; *HC* 249: 7 February 1984 (Current Edition). Updating of the Register is a continuous process and a manuscript copy of the updated Register is available for public inspection at the Registry of Members' Interests.

7 Multiple Standards?

1 E.N. Gladden, *Civil Service of the United Kingdom*, Frank Cass and Co. Ltd, 1967.
2 Prerogative Orders in Council are of a legislative rather than a judicial character and are published as an appendix to the annual volumes of statutory instruments. Unlike legislative Orders in Council they are not statutory instruments.
3 Cited in the *Salmon Commission Report*, Cmnd 6524:1976, p. 165.
4 Granada Television, 'World in Action', 19.7.1976.
5 Rules of the Department of the Environment, cited in Appendix 16 to the *Salmon Commission Report*, Cmnd 6524:1976.
6 Figures derived from the Fourth Report of the Treasury and Civil Service Committee, 'Acceptance of Outside Appointments by Crown Servants', *HC* 216: March 1981.
7 Ibid., para 33.
8 Cited in the *Guardian*, 15.4.1982.

9 Memorandum from the General Secretary of the Society of Civil Servants to the members of the General Purposes Committee of the Society of Civil Servants, July 1974.
10 Cited in the appendix to a First Division Association of Civil Servants internal report (1969) on Professional Standards in the Public Service.
11 Confirmed by communication with the United Grand Lodge of England.
12 Public Records Office, HO 241/72.
13 Dr. Alan Parker, Aidan Rose and John Taylor at Teesside Polytechnic are engaged in a research project that aims to examine the practices and procedures currently employed by local authorities in England and Wales in relation to standards of conduct. Some of the ground for the project is set out in a co-authored article, 'Fishing for Salmon', in *Local Government Studies*, Vol. 9 (Sept/Oct 1983).
14 Commissioners for Local Administration were established under the Local Government Act, 1974, with the task of investigating complaints made by members of the public who feel they have received injustice as a result of maladministration by local authorities.
15 Commission of Local Administration, Report for the year ended 31 March 1981, para 31 (b).
16 *The Times*, 4.7.1973.
17 *Members of Parliament and Conflict of Interest*, Green Paper signed by President of the Privy Council of the Canadian Government, July 1973, p. 6.
18 Houghton, the Rt. Hon. Douglas (now Lord) Houghton, 'Financial Interests of Members of Parliament', *The Parliamentarian*, Vol. LV (1974), p. 7.

8 The Experience of the American Congress

1 The information presented here on Members' allowances was derived from Congressional Quarterly's *Guide to Congress*, third edition.
2 US Commission on Executive, Legislative, and Judicial Salaries, Report, Washington, US Govt. Print. Off., 1977, esp. pp. 26–31.
3 Final Report of the Select Committee on Ethics, House Report No. 95–1837, Ninety-fifth Congress, 2nd Session, 1979, p. 29.
4 *Laxalt vs. Kimmitt*. The Court dismissed this complaint in March 1978. Cross appeals were filed and on 14 January 1983 the US Court of Appeals ordered that the appeal be dismissed because of the Senate's action of 14 December 1982 deleting the outside earned income limitation rule in its entirety.

5 Report of The Select Committee on Official Conduct, To Accompany S. Res. 110, Senate Report No. 95–49, Ninety-fifth Congress, 1st Session, 1977, p. 9.
6 Kenneth Bradshaw and David Pring, *Parliament and Congress*, Great Britain, Quartet Books Ltd, rev. ed. 1981, pp. 112–13.
7 *Congressional Quarterly Weekly Report*, Vol. 38, No. 34, p. 2466, 23 August 1980.
8 Cited in *Congressional Quarterly Weekly Report*, Vol. 41, No. 48, p. 2563, 3 December 1983.
9 Cited in *Congressional Quarterly Weekly Report*, Vol. 41, No. 24, p. 1202, 18 June 1983.
10 Cited in *Congressional Quarterly Weekly Report*, Vol. 41, No. 34, p. 1730, 27 August 1983.
11 Hearings and Markup before the Committee on Rules, House of Representatives, Ninety-fifth Congress, 1st Session on H. Res. 287, 23 and 24 February 1977, p. 122.

9 A Problem of Interest

1 For example, see the argument in *Members of Parliament and Conflict of Interests*. Green Paper signed by President of the Privy Council of the Canadian Parliament, July 1973, pp. 2–3.
2 Ronald Fletcher, *Sociology: The Study of Social Systems*, London, Batsford, 1981, pp. 16–17.
3 *The Times*, 19.7.1972. For a useful discussion of whether political careers can be assessed as a profession, the reader is referred to H. Eulau and J. Sprague, *Lawyers in Politics, A Study in Professional Convergence*, Indianapolis, Bobbs Merrill Co, 1964, pp. 139–141.
4 Michael Pinto-Duschinsky, *British Political Finance 1830–1980*, Washington and London, American Enterprise Institute for Public Policy Research, 1982.

Appendix 1
A Note on Sources

> A major difficulty that faces students of government is the lack of information. This is especially true of Britain where so much public business is conducted in a secretive, club-like atmosphere that is now spreading from Whitehall and Westminster to the powerful pressure groups, especially the trade unions. So the gap is widening between the real world of politics and academic political scientists.[1]

During research for this study a number of sources and methods were combined in order to tackle this fundamental problem of data collection.

In brief, material collected on the British House of Commons fell into two main categories: firstly, parliamentary documentation on Members' interests, which consisted primarily of House of Commons Debates, Parliamentary Questions, Early Day Motions and Select Committee Reports; secondly, responses to both key informant interviews and a small random sample survey of MPs. This was supplemented by some archival material, derived chiefly from Public Records Office files, and facts and opinions on Members' interests culled from newspaper coverage of the issue. Information on the American Congress was derived chiefly from congressional publications, and from congressmen and congressional staff who were kind enough to answer my questions with lengthy correspondence.

This note sets out the major sources of written documentation. My use of the interview technique is explained in Appendix 2.

British government publications Both parliamentary and non-parliamentary publications were consulted. The most widely used House of Commons publications were *Hansard* (the Official Report of the House of Commons), the *Journal of the House of Commons*, and the *Register of Members' Interests*. In addition, all Reports of the Select Committee of Privileges since 1945 were searched for relevant material, as were all *ad hoc* Select Committee Reports concerned in any way with the issue of Members' interests or conduct.

The most systematically analysed was *Hansard*. Sessional and volume indexes were carefully scanned for the period 1945–1983. The resultant compilation of *Hansard* data, covering both Debates and Parliamentary Questions, revealed much about the way parliamentarians view and publicly articulate the issue of conflict of interest.

Hansard also provided the basis for division list analysis. Divisions on the motions and amendments to motions regarding declaration and registration interests which were debated in the House on 22 May 1974 and 12 June 1975 were analysed in order to explore intra- and inter-party differences on the subject of Members' interests (Appendix 4). For the same purpose Early Day Motions relating to Members' interests and the conduct of Members which were tabled during the modern campaign for the Register were analysed. These motions were identified from the House of Commons Library Bound Volumes of Early Day Motions (containing data extracted from 'Notices of Questions and Motions'). Early Day Motions are motions tabled by backbench Members who solicit signatures from their parliamentary colleagues. They are chiefly a device whereby MPs advertise their views, and unless a motion is sponsored by the Government or Official Opposition, it is unlikely to be debated.

A broad criticism of *Hansard* as a data source in parliamentary research is that it is a dispassionate record of what is said in Parliament, and as such takes no account of the mood of the House or the context of events. As argued by Professor G.W. Jones,

> . . . political scientists with their focus on the written word and on what is quantifiable, often neglect the mood, atmosphere and emotional feel of a situation. Hansard, a cold compilation of words spoken, is inadequate as a record of what happened in Parliament. It omits the flavour that needs to be captured from journalists' reports and diaries.[2]

In an attempt to overcome this deficiency, although it can never be eliminated altogether, newspaper reports were used as described below, and where possible biographies, diaries and memoirs were referred to, remembering that these sources possess their own particular shortcomings in the form of potential bias and unrepresentativeness.

Archives The main archival material consulted was that held by the Public Record Office. Because of the 30 year (or longer) retention of official documents under the Public Records Acts, 1958 and 1967, the value of this source of information was largely restricted to the provision of historical background material. The main categories of information which proved relevant to the subject were files of the Prime Minister's Office (PREM), the Cabinet Office (CAB) and the Home Office (HO). In searching for relevant files I would like to acknowledge the help received from the Archival Records Section of both the Cabinet Office and the Home Office.

The Press Newspaper reports are the main documentary basis for historical periods for which official archives are not open, and here they proved particularly helpful in mapping out the campaign for a register of Members' interests. This occurred during the 1960s and early 1970s, when Public Record Office material relevant to this period was closed. In order to reduce inaccuracy and distortion, reports of the same events by national newspapers of different editorial views were compared, and as far as possible the details of the reports were checked with key informants (Appendix 2) who had participated in, or were familiar with, the events in question. The main newspapers consulted were: *The Times, Guardian, Daily Telegraph, Sunday Times, Sunday Telegraph* and *Observer.*

American government publications The co-operation of the staff of the United States Congress in supplying me with free copies of congressional publications was overwhelming. The major publications used are listed in the bibliography. The *Congressional Record* (roughly equivalent to *Hansard*, although it allows revision) was also consulted with a view to obtaining insight into congressional attitudes. In addition to these primary sources of data, an invaluable secondary source was *Congressional Quarterly* (and *Congressional Quarterly Weekly Report*).

Notes

1 Professor F.F. Ridley, *Parliamentary Affairs*, Vol. XXXI (1978), p. 355.
2 G.W. Jones, 'Personalities, Power and Parliament', Book Section, *Parliamentary Affairs*, Vol. XXXII (1979), p. 106.

Appendix 2
A Note on Interview Technique

As these interviews were conducted for my doctoral thesis, the information and perceptions yielded by them relate primarily to the British House of Commons.

Key information interviews

> Concentration on a few key informants may . . . help the investigator to acquire a better picture of the norms, attitudes, expectations of a particular group than he could obtain *solely* from less intensive observations or through conducting a greater number of less intensive interviews, by themselves. Naturally, it will often be preferable to combine the use of informants with other interviewing and with other methods of data collection.[1]

This observation by Lewis Dexter in his study on elite and specialised interviewing provides a useful synopsis of the role of key informant interviewing in this study, with the qualification that here key informant interviews were used to inquire into facts as well as norms and attitudes etc.

In total 25 key informants were interviewed. Apart from a small number who were involved in local government, commercial or professional practice, pressure groups etc., these tended to be drawn from four main areas: the House of Commons Clerks, Members of the House of Commons, Members of the House of Lords, and civil servants from Government Departments.

The method of key informant interviewing performed a complementary role to the random sample survey described below. Used alone, random sample interviewing would not have been sufficient because persons of supposedly equal rank – in this case MPs – may possess different kinds and amounts of information. Also, because of their occupation of a variety of roles in the House some people – for example, Leaders of the House, Chairmen of Select Committees – are able to perceive its operation through a variety of lenses which gives them a unique perspective on Parliament. To have relied on random sample interviewing of MPs would almost inevitably have excluded from the sample persons with special or strategic knowledge of the subject in hand.

To overcome this problem 'experts' were interviewed who were known to possess such knowledge. As each person may have possessed a partial or biased view of the subject a number of informants were selected and their interpretations of events checked one against another. Any person, issues or events that did not 'exist' for any one informant were considered as a possible source of bias in his report. In some cases this potential bias may have derived from forgetfulness. Where possible both documentary and interview material on the same events were collected and compared.

The interviews were conducted between April 1978 and April 1980 inclusive (contact has since been re-established with some respondents in order to update information). Their average length was one and a quarter hours. Most of those who were contacted agreed to be interviewed. The small number of outright refusals or non-responses came mainly from Conservative MPs who then held ministerial office and a few MPs who gave lack of time as the reason for their refusal (some of these did however provide valuable information in the course of lengthy correspondence or telephone conversations). Although small, this non-response may have led to some events being underemphasised because less information was collected on them.

The interviews were 'focused', in that specific topics or questions were intended to be covered, but open-ended questions were often used. This method proved useful where experiences, feelings or motives were involved and where the lack of comparability of one interview with the next did not present insuperable problems.

The random sample survey

This was not the keystone of the research but, in the exploration of MPs' perceptions and opinions concerning conflict of interest, emerged as a necessary adjunct to the extensive documentary research and key informant interviewing that had gone before. For this reason, and because of limited time, it was decided to accept the problems of analysis and generalisability associated with samples of less than 50, and to restrict the survey to 30 Members; roughly a 5 per cent sample of the House of Commons.

The method of random sampling was adopted for the survey.[2] The sample was drawn by the method of 'systematic sampling'; i.e. where the desired sampling fraction is 'k', selecting every kth person throughout the list, starting with a randomly chosen number between one and k inclusive. Bearing in mind that a proportion of those 30 MPs would for various reasons not respond, a second sample of 30 MPs was drawn in exactly the same way as the original sample; the intention being to reach the correctly proportioned target of 30 MPs by systematically working through the names in the second sample until the target number was reached.

A factor which created sampling problems for this study was the calling of a general election in May 1979, precisely at the time when the sample was being drawn. As a large part of the research data was concerned with the campaign for a register of Members' interests, a decision had already been taken that the sample should reflect the composition and climate of opinion in the House in 1974, the year when the House agreed to the motion to introduce the Register. If the general election had not occurred the majority of MPs who had been sitting in the House in 1974 would still have been there. However, at the May election 61 Members took the opportunity to retire from the House, many lost their seats and an influx of new Members entered the House. It was decided that the most appropriate sampling frame would consist of those MPs who had been in the House at the time of the 1974 motion and who were still Members in 1979. This sampling frame did, however, carry the risk of some bias associated with the group of MPs who retired from Parliament (many of whom tended to be of the older generation of MPs aged 60 and above) or those who lost their seats in the May 1979 general election. With regard to the latter group it is likely that there may have been some bias in the sample in favour of safe seats as against, say, Labour marginals.

To increase the precision of the sample as a reflection of the climate of opinion in the House in 1974, the sample was stratified according to voting behaviour in the Division on the motion to establish a Register of Members' Interests (Div. 31 of 22 May 1974). It was felt that voting behaviour (or abstention) in this Division would give some indication, subject to qualifications discussed in the text, of a Member's position on the general issue of Members' interests, and more specifically, the Register. Although this technique increased the chances of creating a representative cross-section of opinion in the House, the warning given by one Conservative MP interviewed serves as a necessary reminder of one of the main problems in trying to interview a representative sample of MPs. Commenting from the experience of variations in his own Party, particularly the differences between new Tories and the old guard, he stressed that MPs have such varied opinions (particularly on non-party issues) that it would be necessary to interview all 635 Members to get a true picture – and as he added, this would not be possible as some MPs make it a point of principle not to assist with any requests for assistance with research, regardless of the subject matter.

MPs' replies to an introductory letter asking for their assistance with the survey confirmed this researcher's assumption that they were inundated with requests for help with research. One MP went so far as to say, 'there has recently been an epidemic, almost amounting to a plague, of requests made by those who are carrying out researches into matters which touch and concern Members of Parliament'. Another MP demonstrated the type of resistance researchers are likely to meet by stressing that, 'all letters from researchers and all "animal" letters go straight into the bin'. What came through strongly from the replies was that MPs were more likely to react favourably to an 'articulate' letter which was personally typed rather than photocopied, and that persistence, in terms of follow-up letters was often necessary to elicit agreement to an interview.[3]

The response rate for the sample as a whole was 57 per cent (although, as explained above, a second sample of MPs was drawn on a random sample basis in order to reach the target number to be interviewed within each stratum). As shown in Table 4, the rates for each of the strata were as follows: Ayes 61 per cent, Noes 50 per cent, Absent/Abstained 56 per cent. Several factors contributing to an explanation of these differences in response rates emerged from the interviews and from letters of refusal. Those who voted to establish the Register tended to be more interested in the subject of research and were more ready to talk about it than those who voted no or abstained. Many of those who voted no or abstained felt they had nothing to contribute on the subject, and even after reassurance that their opinions were equally as valuable as those who had voted yes in gauging the climate of opinion in the House in 1974, some still declined to be interviewed. Closely associated with this explanation was the factor of party. All those in the 'Noes' stratum and the 'Absent/Abstained' stratum were Conservative Members who had a lower response rate than the Labour Members contacted. Similarly the majority of the 'Ayes' stratum (82 per cent) were Labour Members who had the higher response rate. More Conservative than Labour Members are likely to have outside interests and for this reason, among others identified in the text, they are more likely to be antipathetic to the idea of a register. This is not to attribute such a view to all Conservative Members.

Table 4

Response rate for random sample interviews

Strata	Sample Drawn*	Completed Sample	Response Rate %
Ayes	28	17	60.71
Noes	16	8	50.00
Absent/Abstained	9	5	55.56
Total	53	30	56.60

* Total number drawn in order to reach the target number to be interviewed within each stratum. All were drawn on a random sample basis.

Table 5

Analysis of non-response

		Category of Non-Response						Total Non-Response	
Stratum	Number Sampled*	No Reply		Reasoned Refusal		Unreasoned Refusal		Number	% Rate
Ayes	28	2	7.14%	6	21.43%	3	10.71%	11	39.29
Noes	16	0	0	7	43.75%	1	6.25%	8	50.00
Absent/ Abstained	9	0	0	3	33.34%	1	11.11%	4	44.44
Total	53	2	3.77%	16	30.19%	5	9.43%	23	43.40

* Total number sampled in order to reach the target number to be interviewed within each stratum. All were drawn on a random sample basis.

A detailed analysis of non-response is provided in Table 5. Here the category of non-response is broken down into its main components of 'no reply', 'reasoned refusal' and 'unreasoned refusal'.

no reply Only two Members did not reply at all. Both were Labour Members who had voted for the Register in 1974. Significant in terms of their non-response, both abstained or were absent from the debate on the Register in June 1975.

reasoned refusals Thirteen out of the sixteen Members in this category (81 per cent) gave lack of time as a reason for their refusal. This was particularly so of Conservative Members, many of whom were then, with the change of Government, in ministerial positions. Of the remaining three reasoned refusals one was unclear, another explained, 'this is not a specialist interest of mine!', and the third, curiously a Labour Member, felt he had nothing to add to his opinion that 'the clamour for a register came from the unemployable and the envious'.

unreasoned refusals Five Members, three Labour and two Conservative, gave no reason for their refusals but did at least acknowledge receipt of the request for assistance and confirmed their non-response.

In contrast to the key informant interviews the series of random sample interviews did require a high degree of comparability. Therefore the method of structured interviewing was used incorporating a 'structured' or 'standardised' interview schedule, comprising 37 questions (Appendix 3). This ensured that questions were presented to respondents with exactly the same wording and in exactly the same order. However, a degree of flexibility was retained in the schedule by using a mixture of open-ended and closed questions. Closed questions tended to be used where the possible alternative replies were already known or where information collected in earlier stages of the research indicated clear categories of opinion on a subject, or dimensions of the problem which needed to be explored further.

The interviews were conducted during the six-month period of June to November 1979. The average length of the random sample interviews was 55 minutes. Several interviews extended to one-and-a-half hours, while a small number were limited to 30 minutes because of lack of time on the Member's part.

Notes

1 Lewis Anthony Dexter, *Elite and Specialized Interviewing*, Evanston, North-western University Press, 1970, pp. 8–9.

2 For a full description of the technique used the reader is referred to Appendix 1 of the doctoral thesis on which this book is based: *The Conflict of Interest Issue in the British House of Commons: A Practical Problem and a Conceptual Conundrum*, University of London, 1982.

3 For a discussion of my experiences interviewing MPs the reader is referred to a research note, 'A guide to interviewing MPs: how to avoid relegation to the bin', in *Public Administration Bulletin*, No. 45 (August 1984), pp. 44–52.

Appendix 3
Random Sample Survey: the Interview Schedule

The random sample survey interviews involved a structured interview schedule comprising 37 questions. For the sake of brevity this Appendix simply lists the questions in the order in which they appeared on the schedule.[1]

1 In what ways and to what extent do you think the decision in May 1974 to establish a compulsory register of Members' interests signified a change in the attitude of the House of Commons towards disclosure of interests?

2 The 1969 Select Committee on Members' Interests (Declaration) reached its conclusion not to recommend a Register of Members' Interests on the assumption that MPs should be treated no differently than outside citizens. Do you agree with this assumption, or do you think that on entering public life an MP should be prepared to give up some of his privacy in the area of his financial interests and activities?

3 What information do you think the public has a right to know about the financial activities and interests of its legislators outside the House of Commons?

4 Do you agree with the statement made by Edward Short (now Lord Glenamara) in the May 1974 Debate on Members' interests, that a compulsory register was necessary to restore public confidence in Parliament?

5 (a) Do you think that public anxiety over Members' financial interests has been the main factor influencing the change in Parliament's attitude to disclosure of interests?
(b) What other factors do you think influence Parliament's approach to disclosure of interests?

6 Could you give me the main reason for the position you took in the debate on Members' interests on 22 May 1974, and for the way you voted on the motion to establish a compulsory register of Members' interests?

7 Would you have voted for a voluntary register, or would you have preferred the arrangements regarding Members' interests which existed before the May 1974 resolutions to have continued unchanged? (To be asked of those who voted no or were absent or abstained in the above debate.)

8 What do you consider disclosure of Members' financial interests is for?
(a) Pre-coded reasons:
(i) to provide the House with information on any pecuniary interest or other material benefit which an MP may receive and which may be thought to affect his conduct as an MP or influence his activities, speeches or vote in Parliament?
(ii) to provide the general public with such information?
(iii) to protect a Member against any allegations or innuendos which might be made against him?
(b) any other reasons; if so, please state what?

9 Have you ever made a disclosure statement? If so, when and where?

10 Are you satisfied with the categories of registrable interests included in the Register? (show card displaying classifications used in the Register).

11 (a) Do you think any of the existing categories should be excluded?
(b) If so, what?

12 (a) Do you think any further categories should be included?
(b) If so, what?

13 (a) Do you think any other classes of person besides MPs should register their financial interests?
(b) If so, who?

14 (a) Do you think that interests other than financial interests should be declared and/or registered?
(b) If so, what?

15 Do you think that the Register should be enforced by a standing order as suggested by the Select Committee on Members' Interests?

16 (a) In your view, should the House take action against any Member who refuses to register?
(b) If so, what action should be taken?

17 In your opinion, should the Register be statutory rather than set up by a resolution of the House?

18 In the light of experience of the workings of the Register since 1974, if you had to vote for its continuance which way would you vote? Please give reasons for your answer.

19 What interests, if any (apart from those of your constituents in general), do you think an MP may legitimately represent in the House?

20 What, if any, outside interests do you think MPs may legitimately have?

21 In 1971 the Review Body on Top Salaries reached the conclusion that most Members must be considered as working on a full-time basis, and the level of remuneration assessed accordingly. Do you think MPs' salaries and allowances should be calculated on a full-time basis?

22 Are present salary levels satisfactory?

23 Would it be feasible and/or desirable to raise salaries and ban outside employment?

24 (a) It was suggested in the debate on the motion to set up the 1969 Select Committee on Members' Interests (Declaration), and has been endorsed by a recent Select Committee on Procedure, that the House often behaves in a way that might be described as amateur. Do you think this is a fair description?
(b) Can you tell me what you understand by the term 'amateur' in this context?
(c) Conversely, can you tell me what you understand by the term 'professional' in this context?

25 Do you think the House should consist entirely of full-time Members?

26 (a) To what extent do you consider the job of an MP is for yourself a full-time occupation?
(b) Apart from your work as an MP do you have any other paid or unpaid employment?

27 The issue of Members' interests has been considered by both Labour and Conservative Governments to be a House issue rather than a party issue. Do you think MPs view the issue in a similar way, or do you think there is in practice party clustering in terms of attitudes on this subject?

28 Do you consider the topic of disclosure of Members' interests to be part of the wider debate about open government?

29 Can you tell me whether you are in favour of public sound broadcasting of the procedures of Parliament?
30 Can you tell me whether you are in favour of televising the procedures of Parliament?
31 Do you think the issue of Members' financial interests is a domestic matter which should be settled entirely within the House, or do you think it is a subject for wider discussion, drawing on expertise from this country and perhaps from abroad?
32 To what extent do you think that mutual trust among Members is one of the foundations upon which political life is conducted?
33 Do you think MPs should be subject to the corruption laws in their parliamentary capacity as well as in their private capacity, or do you think that parliamentary privilege should continue to regulate MPs' behaviour in their parliamentary capacity as regards allegations of corruption?
34 (a) Can you tell me what you understand by the term 'corruption'?
(b) How far does it overlap with the term 'conflict of interest'?
35 Could you tell me what aspects, if any, of being an MP might provide the opportunity for a potential 'conflict of interest' and possibly corrupt activity?
36 Have you ever been worried about a possible conflict of interest in your own parliamentary career?
37 Did you give up or sell any interests when you entered Parliament to avoid any potential conflict?

Notes

1 A table of frequencies summarising the interview response data is contained in the doctoral thesis on which this book is based: *The Conflict of Interest Issue in the British House of Commons: A Practical Problem and a Conceptual Conundrum*, University of London, 1982.

Appendix 4
Division List Analysis

Table 6

Voting by party on the amendment to the Government's motion, Members' Interests (Declaration) (No. 1)

Party	Ayes		Noes		Absent or abstained		Total
Labour	0	0	287[a]	95.67%	13	4.33%	300
Conservative	221[a]	74.92%	29	9.83%	45	15.25%	295
Liberal	0	0	10	71.43%	4	28.57%	14
Others	0	0	10	43.48%	13	56.52%	23
Whole House	221	34.97%	336	53.16%	75	11.87%	632[b]

Source Derived from *HC Debs* Vol. 874, cols. 553–538, Div. 30, Session 1974, 22 May 1974. Although *Hansard* and *Commons Journal* (1974), p. 143, records 335 Members voting against the amendment, a count of those names listed as voting with 'Noes' totalled 334. This table works with the latter figure.

a Including tellers

b Total of Members eligible to vote. It does not include Mr. Speaker, the Rt. Hon. Selwyn Lloyd (subtracted from 'Others'), Chairman of Ways and Means, the Rt. Hon. G. Thomas (Labour), and First Deputy Chairman of Ways and Means, the Rt. Hon. H.O. Murton (Conservative). These three Members are excluded from voting because of their appointments. At this time there was no Second Deputy Chairman of Ways and Means.

The percentage figures always refer to the percentage within a category of Members voting in a particular way.

Table 7

Voting within the Conservative Party on the amendment to the Government's motion, Members' Interests (Declaration) (No. 1)

Type of Conservative	Ayes		Noes		Absent or abstained		Total
'New' Conservatives[a]	36	65.45%	13	23.64%	6	10.91%	55
'Old' Conservatives[b]	185	77.08%	16	6.67%	39	16.25%	240
Total	221[c]	74.92%	29	9.83%	45	15.25%	295[d]

Source Derived from *HC Debs* Vol. 874, cols. 533–538, Div. 30, Session 1974, 22 May 1974.

a Includes all Conservative Members newly elected to the House at the General Election on 28 February 1974 (*Source: Times Guide to the House of Commons*, February 1974).

b Includes all Conservative Members who were Members before the General Election on 28 February 1974 and who were re-elected.

c Includes tellers

d Total of Conservatives eligible to vote (it excludes the Rt. Hon. H.O. Murton, who, as First Deputy Chairman of Ways and Means is ineligible to vote).

The percentage figures always refer to the percentage within a category of Members voting in a particular way.

Significance test A chi-square test on this table produced a computed value of x^2 = 14.7375 (degrees of freedom = 2). Value of x^2 when P = 0.001 and N = 2 is 13.82.

Therefore, we can say with 99.9 per cent confidence that there is a significant difference in voting behaviour between 'new' and 'old' Conservatives. Those Conservative MPs entering the House at the February 1974 General Election show a greater tendency to vote against the amendment than their colleagues with longer parliamentary service.

Table 8

Voting by Party on the Government's motion, Members' Interests (Declaration) (No. 2), to establish a compulsory Register of Members' Interests

Party	Ayes		Noes		Absent or abstained		Total
Labour	282[a]	94.00%	2	0.67%	16	5.3%	300
Conservative	62	21.01%	168[a]	56.95%	65	22.03%	295
Liberal	10	71.43%	0	0	4	28.57%	14
Others	11	47.83%	0	0	12	52.17%	23
Whole House	365	57.75%	170	26.90%	97	15.35%	632[b]

Source Derived from *HC Debs* Vol. 874, cols. 539–544, Div. 31, Session 1974, 22 May 1974.

a Including tellers

b Total of Members eligible to vote. It does not include Mr. Speaker, the Rt. Hon. Selwyn Lloyd (subtracted from 'Others'), Chairman of Ways and Means, the Rt. Hon. G. Thomas (Labour), and First Deputy Chairman of Ways and Means, the Rt. Hon. H.O. Murton (Conservative). These three Members are excluded from voting because of their appointments. At this time there was no Second Deputy Chairman of Ways and Means.

The percentage figures always refer to the percentage within a category of Members voting in a particular way.

Table 9

Voting within the Conservative Party on the Government's motion, Members' Interests (Declaration) (No. 2) to establish a compulsory Register of Members' Interests

Type of Conservative	Ayes		Noes		Absent or abstained		Total
'New' Conservatives[a]	21	38.18%	26	47.27%	8	14.55%	55
'Old' Conservatives[b]	41	17.08%	142	59.17%	57	23.75%	240
Total	62	21.02%	168[c]	56.95%	65	22.03%	295[d]

Source Derived from *HC Debs* Vol. 874, cols. 539–544, Div. 31, Session 1974, 22 May 1974.

a Includes all Conservative Members newly elected to the House at the General Election on 28 February 1974. (*Source: Times Guide to the House of Commons*, February 1974).

b Includes all Conservative Members who were Members before the General Election on 28 February 1974 and who were re-elected.

c Includes tellers

d Total of Conservatives eligible to vote (it excludes the Rt. Hon. H.O. Murton, who as First Deputy Chairman of Ways and Means is ineligible to vote).

The percentage figures always refer to the percentage within a category of Members voting in a particular way.

Significance test A chi-square test of significance on this table produced a computed value of $x^2 = 12.3409$ (degrees of freedom = 2). Value of x^2 when $P = 0.01$ and $N = 2$ is 9.210.

Therefore, we can say with 99 per cent of confidence that there is a statistically significant difference in voting behaviour between 'new' and 'old' Conservatives. Those Conservative MPs entering the House in February 1974 show a greater tendency to vote for a compulsory register than their colleagues with longer parliamentary service.

Table 10

Voting by party on the Government's motion, Members' Interests (Declaration) (No. 1) to agree with the recommendations made in the Report of the Select Committee on Members' Interests (Declaration)

Party	Ayes		Noes		Absent or abstained		Total
Labour	137[a]	45.97%	1	0.36%	160	53.69%	298
Conservative	33	11.19%	20[a]	6.78%	242	82.03%	295
Liberal	4	28.57%	0	0	10	71.43%	14
Others	9	39.13%	2[a]	8.70%	12	52.17%	23
Whole House	183	29.05%	23	3.65%	424	67.30%	630[b]

Source Derived from *HC Debs* Vol. 893, cols. 799–802, Div. 231, Session 1974/75, 12 June 1975.

a Including tellers

b Total of Members eligible to vote. It does not include Mr. Speaker, the Rt. Hon. Selwyn Lloyd (subtracted from 'Others'), Chairman of Ways and Means, the Rt. Hon. G. Thomas (Labour), First Deputy Chairman of Ways and Means, the Rt. Hon. H.O. Murton (Conservative) and Second Deputy Chairman of Ways and Means, Sir Myer Galpern (Labour). These four Member are excluded from voting because of their appointments. Further, one seat was vacant. A by-election was pending at Greenwich, Woolwich West owing to the death on 19 March 1975 of Mr. W. Hamling (Labour).

The percentage figures always refer to the percentage within a category of Members voting in a particular way.

Select Bibliography

The following bibliography includes the main references I found useful in preparing this book. Not all are referred to directly in the text.

1. Conflict of Interest and Corruption

Chibnall, Steven and Saunders, Peter (1977), 'Worlds apart: notes on the social reality of corruption', *British Journal of Sociology*, Vol. 28, pp. 138–154.

Doig, Alan (1984), *Corruption and Misconduct in Contemporary British Politics*, England, Penguin Books.

Donaldson, Frances (1962), *The Marconi Scandal*, London, Rupert Hart-Davis.

Getz, Robert S. (1966), *Congressional Ethics. The Conflict of Interest Issue*, USA, D. Van Nostrand Co. Ltd.

Heidenheimer, Arnold J. (1970), *Political Corruption. Readings in Comparative Analysis*, USA, Holt, Reinhart and Winston Inc.

Hurstfield, Joel (1967), 'Political Corruption in Modern England: the Historian's Problem', *History*, Vol. 52, pp. 16–35.

Jennings, Sir W. Ivor (1938), 'Corruption and the Public Service', *Political Quarterly*, January 1938, pp. 31–46.

Jones, Professor G.W. (1973), 'Corruption and the Public Interest', *New Society*, 20 September 1973, pp. 703–5.

Kirby, James C. Jr. (1971), *Congress and the Public Trust*, Report of the Association of the Bar of the City of New York Special Committee on Congressional Ethics, New York, Atheneum.

Long, Norton E. (1962), 'Conflict of Interest: a Political Scientist's View', Paper delivered at the Annual Meeting of the American Political Science Association, Washington, September 6–9, 1962.

McGill, Barry (1959), 'Conflicts of Interest: English Experience 1782–1914', *Western Political Quarterly*, Vol. XII, pp. 808–27.

Milne, Edward (1976), *No Shining Armour*, London, John Calder Ltd.

Moodie, Graeme C. (1980), 'On Political Scandals and Corruption', *Government and Opposition*, Vol. 15, pp. 208–22.

Roberts, Michael A., 'The Royal Commission on Standards of Conduct in Public Life 1974–76. Recommendations and Omissions', *Public Administration Bulletin*, No. 23, April 1977.

Scott, James C. (1972), *Comparative Political Corruption*, USA, Prentice Hall.

Senturia, Joseph J. (1931), 'Political Corruption', entry in *Encyclopaedia of the Social Sciences*, Vol. 4, p. 499, New York, The Macmillan Co.

Shackleton, J.R. (1978), 'Corruption: an Essay in Economic Analysis', *Political Quarterly*, Vol. 49, pp. 25–38.

Simpson, Antony E. (1977), *The Literature of Police Corruption*, co-published by the John Jay Press New York and McGraw-Hill Book Co. (UK) Ltd.

Tomkinson, Martin (1973), *Guide to the Poulson Case* (Private Eye Extra), London, Pressdram Ltd.

Tomkinson, Martin and Gillard, Michael (1980), *Nothing to Declare*, London, John Calder.

Vose, Clement (1968), 'Conflict of Interest', entry in *International Encyclopaedia of the Social Sciences*, Vol. 3, p. 242, New York, The Macmillan Co.

Wakfield, Susan (1976), 'Ethics and the Public Service: a Case for Individual Responsibility', *Public Administration Review*, No. 6, pp. 661–66.

Williams, Robert J. (1976), 'The Problem of Corruption: a Conceptual and Comparative Analysis', Paper presented at the Public Administration Committee Conference, York.

Williams, Sandra (1984), 'Observations on Conflict of Interest: a View through the Parliamentary Telescope', *Public Administration Bulletin*, no. 44, April 1984, pp. 47–55.

Williams, Sandra (1983), 'Conflict of Interest: the Experience of the American Congress', *The Parliamentarian*, Vol. LXIV, no. 3, July 1983, pp. 138–45.

Williams, Sandra (1984), 'A Guide to Interviewing MPs: How to avoid Relegation to the Bin', *Public Administration Bulletin*, no. 45, August 1984, pp. 44–52.

Zellick, Graham (1979), 'Bribery of Members of Parliament and the Criminal Law', *Public Law*, Spring 1979, pp. 31–58.

2 Members of Parliament And Their Interests

Beer, Samuel H. (1957), 'The Representation of Interests in British Government: Historical Background', *American Political Science Review*, Vol. LI, pp. 613–650.

Barrington, Hugh (1973), *Backbench Opinion in the House of Commons 1945–55*, Oxford, Pergamon Press.

Birch, A.H. (1964), *Representative and Responsible Government*, London, George Allen and Unwin Ltd.

Birch, A.H. (1971), *Representation. Key Concepts in Political Science*, London, Pall Mall Press.

Boulton, C.J. (1978), 'Conduct of Members', *The Table*, Vol. XLVI, pp. 28–31.

Doig, Alan (1979), 'Self-Discipline and the House of Commons: the Poulson Affair in a Parliamentary Perspective', *Parliamentary Affairs*, Vol. 32, pp. 248–67.

Eulau, H. et al (1959), 'The Role of the Representative:Some Empirical Observations on the Theory of Edmund Burke', *American Political Science Review*, Vol. 53, pp. 742–56.

Hamilton, W.W. (1975), 'Members and Outside Interests', *The Parliamentarian*, Vol. 56–57 (1975–76), pp. 227–31.

Houghton, the Rt. Hon. Douglas (now Lord Houghton) (1974), 'Financial Interests of Members of Parliament', *The Parliamentarian*, Vol. 55, pp. 1–8.

House of Commons Library Research Division Background Paper No. 28, 'The Financial Interests of Ministers and Members of Parliament', 1973, not published.

Judge, David (1980), 'British Representative Theories and Parliamentary Specialisation', *Parliamentary Affairs*, Vol. 33, pp. 40–53.

Judge, David (1981), *Backbench Specialisation in the House of Commons*, London, Heinemann Educational Books.

King, Anthony (1974), *British Members of Parliament: a Self-Portrait*, London, Macmillan Press Ltd. (in association with Granada Television).

Mellors, Colin (1978), *The British MP*, Great Britain, Saxon House.

Muller, William D. (1977), *The 'Kept Men'?*, Great Britain, Harvester Press Ltd.

Newman, Frank C. (1956), 'Reflections on Money and Party Politics in Britain', *Parliamentary Affairs*, Vol. 10 (1956–57), pp. 308–32.

Noel-Baker, Francis (1961), 'The Grey Zone. The Problem of Business Affiliations of Members of Parliament', *Parliamentary Affairs*, Vol. 15 (1961–62), pp. 87–93.

Pitkin, Hanna Fenichel (1972), *The Concept of Representation*, USA, University of California Press.

Richards, Professor Peter G. (1959), *Honourable Members: a Study of the British Backbencher*, London, Faber and Faber.
Richards, Professor Peter G. (1972), *The Backbenchers*, London, Faber and Faber.
Ross, J.F.S. (1948), *Parliamentary Representation*, London, Eyre and Spottiswoode, 2nd edition.
Ross, J.F.S. (1955), *Elections and Electors*, London, Eyre and Spottiswoode.
Roth Andrew et al (1st edition, 1961), *The Business Background of MPs*, London, Parliamentary Profile Services Ltd., further editions published 1963, 1965, 1967, 1972, 1975/6.
Vijay, K.L. (1973), 'The Declaration of Interests by Members of the House of Commons: an Analysis of the Current Campaign for Reform', *Political Quarterly*, Vol. 44, pp. 478–86.
Willey, the Rt. Hon. F.T. (1975), 'The Declaration and Registration of Members' Interests', *The Parliamentarian*, Vol. 56–57 (1975–76), pp. 167–70.
Winnifrith, C.B. (1975), 'Members' Interests', *The Table*, Vol. XLIII, pp. 30–5.
Zellick, Graham (1978), 'The Conduct of Members of Parliament', *Public Law*, Summer 1978, pp. 133–43.

3 General Politics

Anson, Sir William R. (1922), *The Law and Custom of the Constitution, Vol. 1, Parliament*, Oxford at the Clarendon Press, 5th edition.
Bagehot, Walter (1867), *The English Constitution*, London, Fontana/Collins, with introduction by R.H.S. Crossman, 1963 (first published 1867).
Beer, Samuel H. (1971), *Modern British Politics*, London, Faber and Faber.
Blondel, J. (1963), *Voters, Parties and Leaders*, Great Britain, Penguin.
Bradshaw, Kenneth and Pring, David (1981), *Parliament and Congress*, Great Britain, Quartet Books Ltd, rev. ed.
Buck, P.W. (1963), *Amateurs and Professionals in British Politics 1918–59*, Chicago, University of Chicago Press.
Campion, Sir Gilbert (1950), *An Introduction to the Procedure of the House of Commons*, London, Macmillan and Co. Ltd, 2nd edition.
Cartwright, T.J. (1975), *Royal Commissions and Departmental Committees in Britain*, London, Hodder and Stoughton.
Chester, D.N. and Bowring, Nona (1962), *Questions in Parliament*, Oxford, Clarendon Press.

Clifford, F. (1887), *A History of Private Bill Legislation*, Vol. II, London, Butterworth.
Crossman, Richard (1977), *The Diaries of a Cabinet Minister, Vol. 3: Secretary of State for the Social Services, 1968–70*, London, Hamish Hamilton and Jonathan Cape.
Finer, S.E. (1969), *Anonymous Empire. A Study of the Lobby in Great Britain*, London, Pall Mall Press, 2nd edition.
Guttsman, W.L. (1965), *The British Political Elite*, London, MacGibbon and Key, rev. ed.
Harrison, M. (1960), *Trade Unions and the Labour Party Since 1945*, London, Allen and Unwin.
Jennings, Sir W. Ivor (1957), *Parliament*, Cambridge, Cambridge University Press, 2nd edition.
Keeton, George W. (1960), *Trial by Tribunal*, London, Museum Press.
Kilmuir, Viscount (1969), 'The Law of Parliamentary Privilege', a lecture delivered before the University of London, 4 May 1959, University of London, The Athlone Press.
Laski, Harold J. (1938), *Parliamentary Government in England*, London, George Allen and Unwin Ltd.
Marshall, Geoffrey (1979), 'The House of Commons and its Privileges' in Walkland, Stuart (ed.), *The House of Commons in the Twentieth Century*. Oxford, Clarendon Press, ch. 4, pp. 204–46.
Namier, L.B. (1929), *The Structure of Politics at the Accession of George III*, Vol. 1, London, Macmillan.
Norton, Philip (1981), *The Commons in Perspective*, Oxford, Martin Robertson.
O'Leary, Cornelius (1962), *The Elimination of Corrupt Practices in British Elections 1868–1911*, Oxford, Clarendon Press.
Pachauri, P.S. (1971), *The Law of Parliamentary Privileges in U.K. and in India*, New York, Oceana Publications Inc.
Pinto-Duschinsky, Michael (1982), *British Political Finance 1830–1980*, London and Washington, American Enterprise Institute.
Porritt, Edward and Annie (1909), *The Unreformed House of Commons: Parliamentary Representation before 1832*, London, Cambridge University Press.
Redlich, Joseph (1908), *Procedure of the House of Commons*, 3 vols. translated by A.E. Steinthal, Archibald, Constable and Co. Ltd.
Rhodes, Gerald (1975), *Committees of Inquiry*, London, George Allen and Unwin.
Richardson, J.J. and Jordan, A.G. (1979), *Governing Under Pressure: the Policy Process in a Post-Parliamentary Democracy*, Oxford, Martin Robertson.
Rush, Michael (ed.) (1983), *The House of Commons: Services and Facilities, 1972–1982*, London, Policy Studies Institute (no. 614).

Schattschneider, E.E. (1960), *The Semi-Sovereign People: a Realist's View of Democracy in America*, New York, Holt, Rinehart and Winston.

Shils, Edward A. (1956), *The Torment of Secrecy*, London, Heinemann.

Stewart, J.D. (1958), *British Pressure Groups: Their Role in Relation to the House of Commons*, Oxford and New York.

Stewart, Michael (1938), *The British Approach to Politics*, London, George Allen and Unwin Ltd.

Wheare, K.C. (1955), *Government by Committee*, Oxford, Clarendon Press.

Williams, O.C. (1948), *The Historical Development of Private Bill Procedure*, London, H.M.S.O.

Young, R. (1962), *The British Parliament*, London, Faber and Faber.

4 Methodology

Almond, G. and Verba, S. (1963), *The Civic Culture*, USA, Princeton University Press.

Apter, David (ed.) (1964), *Ideology and Discontent*, New York, Free Press.

Bachrach, Peter and Baratz, Morton S. (1962), 'The Two Faces of Power', *American Political Science Review*, Vol. 56, pp. 947–52.

Bachrach, Peter and Baratz, Morton S. (1970), *Power and Poverty. Theory and Practice*, London, Oxford University Press.

Benn, S.I. (1959), '"Interests" in Politics', *Proceedings of the Aristotelian Society*, New Series, Vol. LX (1959–60).

Blondel, J. (1975), 'Plea for Problem-oriented Research in Political Science', *Political Studies*, Vol. 23, pp. 232–43.

Cohen, Percy (1968), *Modern Social Theory*, London, Heinemann.

Crenson, Matthew A. (1971), *The Un-Politics of Air Pollution. A Study of Nondecision-making in the Cities*, Baltimore and London, The John Hopkins Press.

Dexter, Lewis Anthony (1970), *Elite and Specialized Interviewing*, USA, North-western University Press.

Downs, Anthony (1972), 'Up and Down with Ecology – the "Issue-Attention" Cycle', *The Public Interest*, Vol. 28, pp. 38–50.

Duverger, Maurice (1964), *Introduction to the Social Sciences*, London, George Allen and Unwin Ltd.

Fletcher, Ronald (1981), *Sociology: the Study of Social Systems*, London, Batsford.

Galnoor, Itzhak (1977), *Government Secrecy in Democracies*, New York, New York University Press.

Greenstein, Fred I. (1969), *Personality and Politics*, Chicago, Markham Publishing Co.

Lukes, Steven (1974), *Power: a Radical View*, London, The Macmillan Press Ltd.

Mannheim, K. and Stewart, W. (1962), *An Introduction to the Sociology of Education*, Routledge and Kegan Paul.

Mills, C. Wright (1956), *The Power Elite*, New York, Oxford University Press.

Moser, C.A. and Kalton, G. (1973), *Survey Methods in Social Investigation*, London, Heinemann Educational Books, 2nd edition, reprinted 1973.

Patterson, Samuel C. (1973), 'Review Article: the British House of Commons as a Focus for Political Research', *British Journal of Political Science*, Vol. 3 (1973–74), pp. 363–81.

Putnam, Robert D. (1973), *The Beliefs of Politicians*, New Haven and London, Yale University Press.

Pye, L. and Verba, S. (eds) (1965), *Political Culture and Political Development*, USA, Princeton University Press, particularly Rose, Richard, 'England: a Traditionally Modern Political Culture', at pp. 83–130.

Schubert, Glendon (1960), *The Public Interest: a Critique of the Theory of a Political Concept*, USA, The Free Press.

Sellitz, C., Jahoda, M., Deutsch, M., Cook, S. (1965), *Research Methods in Social Relations*, New York, Holt, Rinehart and Winston.

Shils, Edward A. (1970), 'Centre and Periphery', in Worsley, P. (ed.), *Modern Sociology; Introductory Readings: Selected Readings*, Harmondsworth, Penguin, at pp. 415–427.

Sjobert, G. and Nett, R. (1968), *A Methodology for Social Research*, USA, Harper and Row.

Sorauf, Frank J. (1957), 'The Public Interest Re-considered', *Journal of Politics*, Vol. XIX, pp. 616–39.

Stacey, Margaret (1969), *Methods of Social Research*, Great Britain, Pergamon Press.

Subramaniam, V. (1968), 'The relative status of specialists and generalists: an attempt at a comparative historical explanation', *Public Administration*, Vol. 46.

Weber, Max (1949), *Methodology of the Social Sciences*, translated and edited by Edward A. Shils and Henry A. Finch, New York, The Free Press, particularly the essay '"Objectivity" in Social Science and Social Policy', pp. 49–112.

Wilkinson, Rupert H. (1964), *The Prefects. Leadership and The Public School Tradition*, London, Oxford University Press.

5 Reference Works And Guides On Parliament

This list contains only those reference works or guides most widely used for this study.

Butler, David and Sloman, Anne (1980), *British Political Facts 1900–1967*, London, Macmillan, 5th edition.

Dod's Parliamentary Companion, Great Britain, Dod's Parliamentary Companion Ltd, established in 1832, published annually.

Ford, P. and Ford, G. (1955), *A Guide to Parliamentary Papers*, Oxford, Basil Blackwell, rev. ed., Irish University Press, 1972.

Hulke, Malcolm (ed.) (1974), *Cassell's Parliamentary Directory*, London, Cassell.

May, Sir Thomas Erskine, *Parliamentary Practice*, (known as *Erskine May*), London, Butterworths: 19th edition 1976, edited by Sir David Lidderdale, KCB, Clerk of the House of Commons.

Ollé, J.G. (1973), *An Introduction to British Government Publications*, London, Association of Assistant Librarians, 2nd edition.

Pemberton, John E. (1971), *British Official Publications*, London, Pergamon Press.

The Times Guide to The House of Commons, London, Times Books Ltd: the June 1983 edition is the latest in a series which began in 1880.

Vacher's Parliamentary Companion, London, A.S. Kerswill Ltd, established in 1832, published quarterly.

Wilding, Norman and Laundy, Philip (1958), *An Encyclopaedia of Parliament*, London, Cassell and Co. Ltd.

6 Parliamentary Publications

Not all the parliamentary and non-parliamentary papers referred to in the text have been included in this list. Only those dealing wholly or in part with the subject of Members' interests or conduct have been selected. In addition, sessional volumes of *Hansard* for the period 1945–1983 were systematically searched and are extensively noted in the text.

Report from the Select Committee on Members of Parliament (Personal Interest), *HC* 274: 1896.

Report from the Select Committee on the Conduct of a Member, *HC* 5: S 1940–41.

Report from the Select Committee of Privileges, *HC* 85: S 1943–44. Concerning the case of Alderman Robinson and the National Union of Allied and Distributive Workers.

Report from the Select Committee of Privileges, *HC* 118: S 1946–47. Concerning the case of Mr. W.J. Brown and the Civil Service Clerical Association.

First Report (Special) from the Select Committee on Members' Interests (Declaration), *HC* 285: S 1968–69.

Report from the Select Committee on Members' Interests (Declaration), *HC* 57: S 1969–70.

First Report from the Review Body on Top Salaries: *Ministers of the Crown and Members of Parliament*, Cmnd 4836:S 1971–2.

First Special Report from the Select Committee on Members' Interests (Declaration), *HC* 176: S 1974–75.

Report from the Select Committee on Members' Interests (Declaration), *HC* 102: S 1974–75.

Second Report from the Select Committee on Members' Interests (Declaration), *HC* 677: S 1974–75.

Report of the Prime Minister's Committee on Local Government Rules of Conduct, Cmnd 5636:1974.

Report from the Select Committee on Members' Interests, *HC* 479: S 1975–76.

Report from the Royal Commission on Standards of Conduct in Public Life, Cmnd 6524:S 1976–77.

Special Report from the Select Committee on Members' Interests, *HC* 84: S 1976–77.

Report from the Select Committee on Conduct of Members, *HC* 490: S 1976–77.

First Report from the Select Committee on Members' Interests, *HC* 377: S 1979–80.

Second Report from the Select Committee on Members' Interests, *HC* 616: S 1979–80.

Select Committee on Members' Interests, Minutes of Proceedings, *HC* 486: S 1980–81.

Select Committee on Members' Interests, Minutes of Proceedings, *HC* 537: S 1981–82.

Select Committee on Members' Interests, Minutes of Proceedings, *HC* 381: S 1981–82.

Special Report from the Select Committee on Members' Interests, *HC* 330: S 1983–84.

Editions of the Register

First Edition: Register of Members' Interests as on 1 November 1975, *HC* 699

As on 26 May 1976, *HC* 284

As on 5 June 1980, *HC* 617

As on 20 March 1981, *HC* 249

As on 18 January 1982, *HC* 158
As on 17 January 1983, *HC* 172
As on 7 February 1984, *HC* 249

Registration is a continuous process. Registers include interests as at the time of going to press. A manuscript of the updated Register is available for public inspection in the Registrar's office, Registry of Members' Interests.

Canadian Parliament

Members of Parliament and Conflict of Interest Green Paper signed by the President of the Privy Council, July 1973, tabled 27 November 1974.

Note Information on specific points about the House of Commons was obtained from the Public Information Office at the House of Commons, London, SW1A 0AA. Tel. 01 219 4272.

7 United States of America: Congressional Publications

Constitution, Jefferson's Manual and Rules of the House of Representatives of the United States, Ninety-fifth Congress.
Senate Manual, containing the Standing Rules, Orders, Laws, and Resolutions affecting the Business of the United States Senate.
Hearings and Markup before the Committee on Rules, House of Representatives, Ninety-fifth Congress, first session on H. Res. 287, 23 and 24 February, 1977.
Report of the Select Committee on Ethics, to accompany H.R.7401, Legislative Branch Disclosure Act of 1977, House Report No. 95–574, Ninety-fifth Congress, first session, 1977.
Report of the Select Committee on Official Conduct, to accompany S.Res.110, Senate Report No. 95–49, Ninety-fifth Congress, first session, 1977.
US Commission on Executive, Legislative, and Judicial Salaries. Report, Washington, US Govt. Print. Off., 1977.
Ethics In Government Act of 1978. Public Law 95–521–October 26 1978, (S555–PL95–521) Ninety-fifth Congress.
Ethics in Government Act of 1978 Amendment. Public Law 96–19 June 1979, Ninety-sixth Congress.
Final Report of The Select Committee on Ethics, House Report No. 95 –1837, Ninety-fifth Congress, second session, 1979.
Congressional Research Service, The Library of Congress. 'Brief History of The Senate Ethics Committee and Code of Conduct', Mildred Amer, Analyst in American National Government, 17 September 1980.

Ethics Manual for Members and Employees of the US House of Representatives. Prepared at the Direction of the Committee on Standards of Official Conduct, Ninety-seventh Congress, first session, 1981.
Rules of Procedure, Committee on Standards of Official Conduct, US House of Representatives, adopted 27 January 1983, Ninety-eighth Congress.

Index